The GARDEN BIRD YEAR

A SEASONAL GUIDE TO ENJOYING THE BIRDS IN YOUR GARDEN

ROY BEDDARD

Illustrations by **DAVID DALY**

Photography by **DAVID COTTRIDGE**

Foreword by
BILL ODDIE

NEW HOLLAND

This edition published in 2009 by New Holland Publishers (UK) Ltd
London • Cape Town • Sydney • Auckland
www.newhollandpublishers.com

Garfield House, 86–88 Edgware Road, London W2 2EA, United Kingdom

80 McKenzie Street, Cape Town 8001, South Africa

Unit 1, 66 Gibbes Street, Chatswood, NSW 2067, Australia

218 Lake Road, Northcote, Auckland, New Zealand

10 9 8 7 6 5 4 3 2 1

ISBN 978 1 84773 503 4

Publishing Director: Rosemary Wilkinson
Publisher: Simon Papps
Editor: Cosima Hibbert
Design: Alan Marshall
Cover Design: Neal Cobourne
Index: Janet Dudley
Production: Joan Woodroffe

Reproduction by Modern Age Repro Co. Ltd, Hong Kong
Printed and bound by Times Offset (M) Sdn Bhd

CONTENTS

FOREWORD

I make television pro-grammes. The BBC does audience research. Thus did I discover that nearly 90 per cent of the regular viewers of *Birding with Bill Oddie* when faced with the question 'do you con-sider yourself a birdwatch-er?' ticked the answer 'no'. However, much the same percentage – and I dare say most of the same people – when asked 'do you enjoy and feed the birds in your garden?' answered 'yes'. I think what we have here is a contradiction in terms!

Ok, we, you – possibly even I – may think of a 'real bird watcher' as one who totes expensive binoculars and a telescope and races round the country chasing rarities (actu-ally, I'd call them a 'twitcher') but how often does that kind of activity involve little more than 'ticking off' the birds, rather than really and truly watching them? The fact is, I honestly do believe that it is in the garden that bird watching in the truest sense of the word takes place. It is here that people get to know not only the various species, but also indi-viduals, as they witness the interaction, the relation-ships, the joys and the tragedies of birds that are truly part of our own lives. People talk about 'their' birds, as if they are friends or neighbours. Indeed they are. What is going on out there is an avian soap opera, and of course soap operas are invariably top of the ratings!

Sorry about the con-stant TV references, but I'm going to finish with another one. We all know that gardening pro-grammes are – how can I put this? – well, there are an awful lot of them – and heaven knows I'm not knocking them – but let me just say that what you will find in this book is rather less about 'decking and ornamental water features', and all about attracting more birds to your garden. It will also allow you to identify them and to understand what they are doing, and – most valuable of all – it will help you discover more about them for yourselves. And that's what I call birdwatching!

Have fun.

THE WILDLIFE TRUSTS

The Wildlife Trusts partnership is the UK's leading voluntary organisation, working, since 1912, in all areas of nature conservation. We are fortunate to have the support of more than 343,000 members, including some famous household names, such as our vice president Bill Oddie.

The Wildlife Trusts protect wildlife for the future by managing in excess of 2,300 nature reserves, ranging from woodlands and peat bogs, to heath lands, coastal habitats and wild flower meadows. We campaign tirelessly on behalf of wildlife, even in garden centres. With other leading environmental organisations, we continue the fight to persuade gardeners to boycott peat and limestone pavement – both vital habitats for many threatened species.

We advise landowners, work to influence industry and government, and run thousands of events and projects for adults and children across the UK. Our junior club Wildlife Watch is also active, with more than 20,000 young environmentalists.

Our Wildlife Gardening initiative encourages people to take action for wildlife in their own back gardens. Readers may have picked up one of our wildlife gardening leaflets or may have seen The Wildlife Trusts Garden at BBC Gardeners' World Live, at the NEC. Visitors to our award-winning show garden included several species of birds, and dragonflies, as well as celebrity gardeners Alan Titchmarsh and Charlie Dimmock.

As traditional wildlife habitats in the countryside come under threat as a result of modern farming techniques, development and water abstraction, gardens are becoming increasingly important. Gardens today are havens for many species of birds – from the familar Green Woodpecker and Swallow to the rarely seen Hoopoe – providing food, shelter and breeding grounds as well as links to urban parks and other open spaces.

Many of the 46 Wildlife Trusts which together make up The Wildlife Trusts partnership, employ staff and volunteers to advise people on how best to encourage wildlife to their back yards. London Wildlife Trust even managed to persuade the Prime Minister Tony Blair to make space for a child-friendly wildlife pond in the garden at Number 10, Downing Street. It is amazing what a difference a few plants, logs or a pond can make to our wildlife, benefiting species as diverse as the Song Thrush, Painted Lady butterfly, Common Frog or Hedgehog.

Thank you for reading Roy Beddard's *The Garden Bird Year* and taking the time to learn about and enjoy the birds on your doorstep.

The Wildlife Trusts is a registered charity (number 207238). For membership, and other details, please phone The Wildlife Trusts on 01636 677711.

INTRODUCTION

As modern farming methods have made large swathes of the countryside less attractive to wildlife, gardens have become vitally important to birds. Populations of many common species have crashed in recent years due to the loss and destruction of their wider habitat, so there has never been a time when birds have been more in need of the food and shelter to be found in the country's gardens.

Changes to the countryside have had a devastating effect on some of our most common birds. In the last fifty years some 300,000 miles of hedgerow have been grubbed up, stubble fields have become a thing of the past and increased use of chemicals has greatly reduced numbers of insects and other invertebrates. Recent studies published jointly by the RSPB and the BTO, *The State of the UK's Birds 2007*, paint an alarming picture of declining populations of birds such as Linnet, Song Thrush, Tree Sparrow and even House Sparrow.

Driven out of the countryside, birds are turning in ever greater numbers to gardens for food and shelter. Gardens throughout northern Europe have become a vital resource for birds and other wildlife. No matter how small or badly located your garden, there is always something you can do to improve it for wildlife. This can consist of feeding birds and other animals or developing and managing the garden to provide natural food and shelter on a more permanent basis.

Something for everyone

Gardens vary enormously by virtue of their size, location and a variety of other factors. This book offers ideas and tips to improve most gardens in a way that

A mature garden is a haven to many species of wild birds, mammals, insects and plants.

will benefit wildlife, and offer something to anybody with a garden.

The book is structured so that it can be used at any time of the year and it has been split into seasonal sections. There is a consistent thread running through these sections that will help you to trace a topic through different seasons. The spring section comes first in the book and this is expanded to give an introduction to the various topics.

There is no single solution that will work in all cases and the subject is too big to give solutions that will satisfy all gardens and all situations. So my intention is to give some basic ideas about feeding birds and gardening for wildlife that can then be applied to a particular situation.

If more detail on a particular subject is required, the list of additional reading and sources of information on page 124 should help to provide the answer to any particularly knotty problem.

Many of us, myself included, in addition to having a love for nature are also keen gardeners. This does not necessarily imply a conflict between garden horticulture and wildlife - compromise is possible. It is not necessary always to use chemicals to solve garden problems - an organic and wildlife-friendly alternative usually exists.

Above: *The cone-like fruits of alders are favoured by seed-eaters such as Redpoll and Siskin in the winter.*

Leaving a space for birds and other creatures may mean your garden is slightly more 'messy' than those at Chelsea, but the increased amount of wildlife interest will more than compensate. The size and location of your garden will place an absolute limit on the bird species it will attract. However, to make the most of any plot, make sure you provide food, water and shelter for birds. Details on how to provide these three essentials can be found in the four seasonal chapters.

Which birds to expect?

The location of your garden is the most important factor in determining which birds might visit. Where exactly is it situated? Coastal or inland? Lowland or upland? City,

Below: *Rosehips are a valuable food source for wild birds, providing nutrition throughout the winter.*

town, village or country? Many of the species accounts refer to the geographical distribution of the particular bird. This will suggest how likely you are to see it in your garden.

I have chosen to include sixty species of birds as those most likely to visit your garden or the area immediately adjacent. These will be the ones that might benefit from changes you make to your garden. Some are resident, some summer visitors and some are occasional winter visitors. Accounts of these different birds are spread across the seasonal chapters depending on when they are most likely to be seen or are showing some particularly interesting behaviour.

The sixty birds mentioned above excludes others that you will see from time to time, which will usually be flying over *en route* to another location. These may include gulls, waders, wildfowl and others. Keeping an eye on these will give you an insight into other fascinating aspects of birdwatching, such as migration and cold weather movements.

If you see most of your garden birds from your kitchen then make sure that you keep a pair of binoculars handy for watching the birds. If you want to record the different species that are seen or what they are doing also keep a notebook and pencil with the binoculars.

Keep a list

Keen birdwatchers are inveterate list keepers and probably the very first thing that you can do is to start to keep a list of the birds you see in your garden. Apart from being a bit of fun this can also help you to keep a check on the effectiveness of the changes you are making to the plants or food available in your garden. New species to your garden will probably be there because of things that you have done. Make a note of the date of your sighting.

The basic garden list can be enlarged to include those birds that you can see from your garden but are not actually in it. This might include gulls or herons flying over on their way to and from a feeding area or a roost site. Alternatively, it might involve keeping a record of the birds using a field you can see from your garden.

Going a step further than a simple list could involve recording

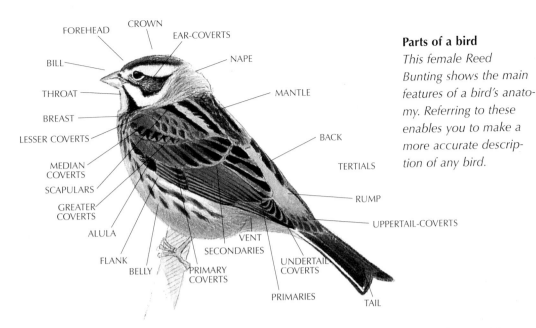

FOREHEAD
CROWN
EAR-COVERTS
BILL
NAPE
THROAT
MANTLE
BREAST
BACK
LESSER COVERTS
TERTIALS
MEDIAN COVERTS
SCAPULARS
RUMP
GREATER COVERTS
UPPERTAIL-COVERTS
ALULA
VENT
FLANK
SECONDARIES
BELLY
UNDERTAIL COVERTS
PRIMARY COVERTS
PRIMARIES
TAIL

Parts of a bird
This female Reed Bunting shows the main features of a bird's anatomy. Referring to these enables you to make a more accurate description of any bird.

how many of a particular species you see. This is another way of checking if your new feeders or berry bushes are attracting more birds. Studying or just watching bird behaviour is fascinating and helps to build up your knowledge of your garden visitors.

Equipment and guides

The only kit a garden birdwatcher needs is a pair of binoculars and a field guide. The range of binoculars available is enormous and so are some of the prices! However, for garden birdwatching there is a wide variety of reasonably priced, easy-to-use binoculars. For use from a house or in a garden the ideal size is about 8x30. The 8 refers to the magnification and the 30 to the size of the front lens. Binoculars of this size will give a bright clear image and will be light for easy handling. The best plan is to visit an optical shop specializing in binoculars and telescopes. Take a birdwatching friend with you if you are unfamiliar with binoculars, and look through a number of pairs to find the one that suits you. A final tip: don't be tempted by the cheaper zoom binoculars sometimes advertised in the classified columns. The magnification is far too high, they will be very difficult to use in the hand and you will be disappointed with the result.

Finally, a field guide is essential, there are many good ones available at reasonable prices. Several are listed in the further reading section of this book and should be available from your local bookshop.

Inevitably a time will come when you see a bird in your garden that you don't recognize! Don't just reach for your field guide. First looking carefully at the bird's size and structure. How big is it? Is it a small songbird

or something larger? Compare it with something you know, e.g. is it Blackbird size? What shape is it? Is it like a finch or a thrush? What shape and size is its bill? Does it walk or hop? Now look closer at its colour and plumage. You could then write a description and try a small sketch if your drawing is up to it. The illustration above shows what the various parts of a bird are called. It might sound a bit complicated but with a bit of practice you will be able to write a fair description. Then you will be ready when an unusual bird, maybe even a rarity, turns up in your garden.

BTO Garden BirdWatch

If you feel that your interest has progressed sufficiently and you would like to contribute to a larger scale study then the BTO (British Trust for Ornithology) runs a project called Garden BirdWatch that might be just the thing for you. Anyone in the British Isles with access to a garden can take part. Month by month, contributing observers send in details of the birds they have been seeing in their gardens. From these individual sightings the BTO compiles an important scientific record of the birds visiting our gardens and how they may be changing. There is a small annual subscription (£15) made by participants which goes towards the cost of running the scheme and in return there is a quarterly newsletter. There is a *Garden BirdWatch Book* available which summarizes the results so far of the survey by species. The most recent edition was published in 2003. The introductory pack for new participants includes this handbook, the news letter and a bird recording pack. For further details see page 124.

Spring

Spring is a season of blossom, birdsong and breeding: returning migrants bring new life to the garden, as courtship and nesting get underway.

To a gardener the spring is one of the most exciting times of the year. If you are not only a gardener but also have an interest in birds, then this is doubly true. As well as watching for the latest flowers to bloom, you are looking out for summer visitors returning from the south to breed. For a gardener the process starts much earlier, when the first very early spring bulbs come out at the beginning of the year. From then onwards there is a succession of delights, with snowdrops and crocuses being followed by daffodils and tulips and all the other plants that make an English spring garden so memorable. In parallel with these plant happenings a gardening birdwatcher is aware of the departure of winter visitors such as Redwings and eagerly awaits the sight of the first Swallow. Then, in early May, comes the sound of the returning Swifts screaming overhead, telling you that summer is just around the corner. By this time, breeding, for the earlier arrivals, is well under way and the garden is full of birds displaying, building nests and singing. A sunny garden early on a May morning takes some beating!

Above: A garden with mature large conifers will often attract breeding Goldcrest. Right: The diminutive Lesser Spotted Woodpecker is an unusual garden breeder, nesting in holes in tree-trunks.

Wildlife gardening

So what is it that birds are looking for? It comes down to three relatively simple requirements: the provision of food and water and the availability of shelter for nesting, roosting and as cover from predators. The things we do in our gardens to improve them for birds will benefit all forms of wildlife.

The key to making a garden attractive to birds in the widest sense is to provide a range of habitats that will meet the three main requirements in different seasons. Food should be available both from natural and artificial sources at all times of the year – these days the provision of food at bird-tables in summer is regarded as a useful supplement to that from natural sources. Planting to ensure a supply of natural food, as well as shelter and nest sites, is a key element in gardening for wildlife, as is the provision of water, which of course also makes an attractive garden 'feature'.

The cultivation regime should be as organic as possible, with natural fertilizers and pesticides being used. Any chemicals that are used should be wildlife friendly. Lawns should be allowed to grow with a modicum of worm-casts and decorative 'weeds'.

Trees, shrubs and climbers

Not every garden has enough space for a tree or two, but many have space for a small one and an existing old gnarled apple is a great asset for the wildlife gardener. Not all trees are slow-growing – I planted several rowan, silver birch and alder 'whips' (small immature trees 0.5–1 m high) and these reached a useful height in five years. Native trees are preferred to exotic species because animal life has evolved to make the most use of them and birds are provided with nest sites, shelter and food at various times of the year.

If there is no space for trees, then a few well chosen shrubs are invaluable. These can be planted in the soil or if space is really at a premium then it is possible to grow them in containers. One of the best is the hawthorn – this provides valuable berries in autumn and if carefully clipped can be dense enough to keep out the most determined predator. The slower growing conifers are also very useful as providers of year-round cover and as a rich source of insects. Finally, although control can be a problem, climbers such as ivy, clematis and honeysuckle give shelter and are an excellent food source.

Suggested trees
- Oak – very large, slow-growing, valuable source of insects and acorns.
- Beech – very large, slow-growing, source of seeds (beechmast)
- Alder – medium/large, fast-growing, shelter and seeds
- Birch – medium, fast growing, shelter and seeds, ornamental
- Apples/pears/wild cherry – small, slow/medium growth, shelter, fruit and insects

Left: *A wildlife garden containing trees, shrubs and a lawn provides a wide range of different habitats.*

Shrubs and climbers
- Berberis – Small/medium, berries, good cover, range of types, can be pruned
- Buddleia – Small/medium, good for insects, decorative, should be pruned
- Cotoneaster – Small/medium, berries, good cover, range of types, can be pruned
- Elder – Small/medium, berries, good for insects, can be pruned
- Hawthorn – Small/medium, berries, good cover, can be pruned

Lawns, weeds and the 'wild-patch'

A well managed lawn can be an invaluable asset to a wildlife garden, and will be used by thrushes, doves and pigeons, Robins and Dunnocks foraging along the edges. It will be a focus of activity all year round. It is better both for the wildlife and the lawn if the cultivation regime is somewhat relaxed, with the blade set higher, cutting less frequent and some weeds being tolerated. Flowering daisies and clover can look very attractive. A little fertilizer is permitted but herbicides and pesticides should be avoided to allow insects and worms to flourish and provide a food source.

There is a wide range of plants that gardeners can grow both for their horticultural value and also for wildlife. During the growing season, they can be a valuable source of insects and when they die back in autumn and winter they should be left so that their seeds and berries will continue to provide food. Wildlife gardens are usually 'messier' than some gardeners will be prepared to tolerate but if space and your gardening pride permit then a 'wild patch' can be valuable for all sorts of wildlife. A range of weeds can be beneficial and as native species they are tailor-made for our wild birds, which are specialists at exploiting them.

- Cow parsley – Seeds and cover for insects
- Dandelion – Seeds
- Groundsel – Seeds and insects
- Knapweed – Seeds and insects
- Nettles – Very good for insects, caterpillars

Above: *A small group of Silver Birch provides winter food for Siskins and Redpolls as well as cover and insects for other species throughout the year.*

- Teasel – Seeds and insects
- Thistle – Seeds, good for insects, ornamental versions can be less invasive

Water and ponds

A source of fresh water is essential for birds throughout the year. If space allows, a pond stocked with suitable aquatic plants is an exellent addition to the garden's range of habitats. Even in small gardens water should be provided in a birdbath or some similar container (and changed regularly). This topic is covered in more detail on pages 17–21.

Feeding garden birds

In order to maximize the number of bird species that visit your garden, it is important to make food available in a range of locations to suit different species' feeding strategies. Many birds prefer feeding on the ground or taking food scattered freely on a flat surface. This is called 'loose feeding' and can be incorporated into a garden feeding station by reserving an area of lawn or border for this style of feeding.

Above: *Conventional bird tables should be uncovered, of decent size, and placed at sufficient height with nearby cover.*

Loose feeding

In suburban areas open feeding stations will often attract feral pigeons. These birds can drive off the smaller species. However, the plus side of attracting large groups of chaffinches and other ground feeders makes it worthwhile. A wider range of foods can be provided at such feeding stations, including kitchen scraps and dried or windfall fruit, especially to attract thrushes in the autumn.

In summer, young nestlings are often fed exclusively by their parents on caterpillars and other small insects, so a bowl of live food such as mealworms placed on the ground or on a bird table can make a welcome treat. In late spring, when a spell of cold or wet weather makes it difficult for birds to collect sufficient insects, provision of live food in this way can be very important. Even when it is not provided, there is some evidence that adults continue to eat seeds and nuts, and feed insects to their nestlings. In the past it was recommended that you should not put out peanuts during the nesting period for fear of nestlings choking. If this is still of concern then once the young birds have fledged and left the nest, a wider range of foods can be safely offered.

A bird table is relatively easy to construct and should be based on a 12 mm thick piece of plywood, which is 45 cm square. This should be placed on a stout pole at least 1.5 m above the ground. The other main consideration is safety from predators, in particular domestic cats. To this end, location is critical – the table should be at least 2 m away from the sort of vegetation that would hide a stalking cat. However, a site next to a perch and some cover such as a holly bush can be beneficial.

Left: *Several thrush species enjoy feeding on apples provided on the lawn during autumn.*

Basic bird feeders

There are two basic types of feeder and these should form the basis of any garden feeding station. The first contains peanuts, and this consists of a wire mesh cylinder fitted with perches and closed at top and bottom with either plastic or metal caps. The other is for dispensing a variety of seeds and is based on a transparent polycarbonate tube fitted with feeding ports and again capped in either metal or plastic. Both designs are hung either from a tree or shrub or are integrated into a garden feeding station Black sunflower seeds have become extremely popular and are eaten by a wide range of garden birds. High-energy formulations and also additives such as oystershell grit are used especially during the breeding season. (The grit helps in eggshell formation.) Feeders must be cleaned often during periods of high usage, and they should be disinfected occasionally.

Metal and plastic feeders are equally effective with one major exception. If grey squirrels are present then metal caps, bases, perches and feeding ports must be used otherwise the feeders will be very quickly destroyed. In the case of the nut feeders, the wire mesh should be made from stainless steel for preference. In my experience such a construction will deter the majority of squirrels.

However, for the very occasional 'super-squirrel' more elaborate constructions are available. Perhaps the simplest of these is a cage where the feeder is constructed as normal but is contained within a ring of steel bars narrow enough to keep out a squirrel but sufficiently wide to allow small birds safe passage.

Both basic types of feeder are available in a wide range of sizes. They hold from 500 g food or less, up to 2–3 kg in the case of the larger seed feeders. For those that want to feed birds on a grand scale there are seed hoppers that hold from 3–6 kg of feed. Conventional wisdom suggests the use of these larger feeders if you are not in a position to replenish them daily. My own experience is that these larger feeders also pull in far larger numbers of birds and mine run out of seed almost as fast as the smaller capacity products.

The final consideration is when to feed during the year. Opinions have changed somewhat in recent years on this topic. There is now evidence that the birds that we encourage to breed in our gardens enjoy lower breeding success than those in more natural habitats and that this is largely due to the poorer food supply. So nowadays the recommendation is to feed all year round, perhaps with the possible addition of live food during the breeding season, and to reduce the feeding from late August to early October when there is an abundance of natural food.

Two conventional forms of feeder: wire mesh cylinders holding peanuts are ideal for tits (below), *while clear tubes with access ports for seeds* (above) *are suitable for less agile species such as House Sparrows.*

Other types of feeders

In order to increase the variety of feeding methods it is possible to provide food in a range of other types of feeder. These often have the aim of attracting a particular species.

A hanging log can be drilled and the holes and cracks in the bark filled with a seed and crushed peanut mix bound together with fat. This will attract a range of tit species and very often a Great Spotted Woodpecker, although in my garden these birds will readily use wire mesh feeders. A traditional way of attracting tits is with a ceramic tit-bell. This is filled with a mixture of fat, nuts and seeds and suspended from a tree or the bird table. A half coconut makes an effective alternative to a tit-bell. Bird cakes can also be made from the same mixture, for which numerous recipes abound (see box right). In winter the temperature allows a more solid mix that is fashioned into blocks and contained in wire-mesh baskets.

Above: *In cold weather bird cake can be fashioned into blocks and offered in wire-mesh baskets.*

It is possible to buy small versions of seed or peanut feeders fitted with suckers suitable for attaching them to a window. Red plastic mesh feeder bags supposedly attract Siskins. However, my experience is that if the birds are present then a standard peanut feeder will

BIRD CAKE RECIPE

- Fill a suitable container or bell with a mixture of ⅔ bird-cake mix and ⅓ melted suet or cooking fat

- Cake mix can contain peanuts (crushed or ground), dried fruit, seeds, oats, cheese and cake crumbs as available

- Cake mix should not contain vegetable matter.

- Allow fat to cool, and when set hang container up from suitable perch

Blue Tits and Great Tits will feed from a bell filled with nuts and seeds set in fat.

be fine. Kitchen scraps are often put on the garden feeding station but can present problems if vermin such as mice or rats are present. In this case the scraps can be contained within a wire-mesh basket or even a disused hanging basket.

The variety of feeders available is very large and readers wishing to see a full range should study the catalogue of one of the suppliers of seeds and feeders listed in the useful addresses on page 124.

Left: *A tray of food attached with a suction pad to a window brings birds really close.*

Water in the garden

Along with food and shelter, water is the third of the ingredients essential in a good bird garden. Birds need water not only for drinking but also for bathing – a good regular supply of fresh water is a key factor in keeping their feathers in tip-top condition. Additionally, in the summer, water can be important in helping birds to keep cool.

The traditional bird bath on a classical stone column is decorative, very expensive but not necessarily the best option for birds. A better way of providing water is in the form of a pond or a simple floor-standing bird bath.

A pond can be both a valuable bird habitat and also a fascinating garden feature in its own right, providing hours of delight and interest for the garden birdwatcher. Birds will come to drink and bathe, hedgehogs will find their way to it, and beautiful floating or marginal water plants make a home for aquatic insects as well as the local frogs, toads and newts. The following pages give tips on how to construct a garden pond and what sort of plants to grow there.

However, not every garden has sufficient space for a pond. In this instance, a bird bath will satisfy many of the birds' needs. Ideally, the bath should have a shallow and a deep end. The shallow end would be used by the smallest birds, while the deeper end which should be a maximum of 7–9 cm deep will be for thrushes and doves wishing to bathe. The best material is either stone or concrete, both of which afford a good grip.

Water in a bird bath quickly gets dirty and in the summer, especially, it should be changed every day. The bird bath should also be cleaned frequently, as algae quickly build up. In the winter it is important to keep the water free of ice during very cold weather. A tennis ball left in the water makes ice easier to remove once the ball is lifted out.

An acceptable alternative to a stone bird bath can be made from a plastic dustbin lid, turned upside down and either sunk into the soil or propped up by house bricks. Another container, that can be used as a cheap bird bath, is a large terracotta dish like those used as a base for a large flower pot.

Below: *A large garden pond with natural banks is a focus for both gardening and wildlife.*

Pond construction

A pond in your garden will provide an important refuge as well as hours of birdwatching and gardening pleasure. To construct a simple pond you will need the following tools and materials:

- Spade
- Spirit-level (900 mm builders level is preferable)
- 10–20 wooden stakes (depends on pond size)
- A length of rope (equal to pond circumference)
- A length of timber (2–3 m, depends on pond size)
- Pond liner
- Underlay or sand/old newspapers

Several different lining materials are available, ranging from black polythene, the cheapest, to butyl rubber, the most expensive. There is a major difference in expected life, with the butyl liner lasting 15–20 years and the polythene perhaps five years.

Site selection and excavation

The first step is to select a suitable site. It is important to find an area that is level and not overshadowed by trees, which will cut down the sunlight and give problems in autumn with falling leaves. Haning chosen a site, use the rope to mark out the outline until you find a shape you are happy with – an irregular oval or kidney shape often works well. With the stakes, mark out the outline more permanently, using four of them to show the longest and widest sections. Make allowance for some shallow shelves on which to place the marginal plants, and also the edging if you want to use flagstones. A better option for wildlife is to have natural banks with a shallow pebble beach in one section but still with built-in marginal shelves.

Remove the turf first, keeping sufficient back for the edging if you are to have natural banks. Next excavate the marginal shelving, allowing a width of 22–30 cm and depth of about 22 cm below the planned water level. If you are edging the pond with flagstones, use the piece of timber and the spirit level to ensure that the tops of the wooden stakes are level. These should be hammered in to mark the planned top surface of the flagstones. When digging out, put the topsoil to one side for future use elsewhere in the garden. Unless you have plans for further major projects, the subsoil can be disposed of in a skip. Plan for a minimum depth of 45 cm and up to a metre for a larger pool. A portion of the perimeter should be shallow, with a depth of 2–10 cm.

Underlay and lining

Once the hole has been excavated, remove any stones or objects that might damage the liner. Spread a layer of damp sand 2–3 cm thick over the entire pond as further protection for the liner. An alternative is damp newspaper, which should be made up to a similar thickness. A

Below: A fibrous synthetic underlay helps protect the liner from sharp stones and roots. Once lined, fill the pond using a hose (below, right), smooth out wrinkles as the water level rises and allow a margin for the edge.

commercially produced fibrous underlay is available and could be considered if roots are a potential hazard.

The size of the liner required for a given pool can be calculated as follows:

Liner length = Maximum Pool Length + twice Maximum Pool Depth

Liner Width = Maximum Pool Width + twice Maximum Pool Depth

An additional 40 cm should be added to both dimensions to allow for a 20 cm overlap with the flagstones or turf.

Filling and finishing off

The liner can now be put into position. Starting at the deepest end, overlap the edge by 20 cm and anchor the liner temporarily with heavy stones. Spread the liner over the remainder of the pond, carefully pushing it into the hole and the corners. Place other stones all around the edge. Using a hose, start to fill the pond. Wearing wellingtons, stand in the rising water to smooth out the wrinkles in the liner as much as possible. When the pond is full, check the perimeter level once more and make final adjustments by adding or removing soil from under the edge of the liner, The pond should be left for a couple of days to settle. Trim

The pond of your dreams? A huge garden pond with luxuriant developing vegetation (above) *may even attract the occasional Heron* (below).

the liner, leaving 20 cm all round as overlap. The edge of the pond can be completed using both soil and retained turf for a natural finish or edging stones held in place with mortar, taking care to keep any mortar out of the pond.

The only other decision to make is whether to contain plants in planting baskets or to cover the bed of the pond with topsoil and plant directly into it. If you choose the latter option, a layer of several inches of soil will be required.

Finally, add a bucket of water and mud from a nearby mature pond, and you will soon find that your new pond is colonised by insect larvae and other aquatic creatures.

A well-stocked pond should hold a variety of marginal and surface plants (above). In muddy shallows these can include the fringed water-lily (below), with its small lily-like leaves and dainty yellow flowers held clear of the water.

Plants for ponds

A pond requires a number of different types of plant to establish a balanced ecological system. The right mix of plants will oxygenate the water and remove excess carbon dioxide. They will also provide food for aquatic creatures, and shelter from the sun and from predators.

Oxygenators

Oxygenators should be introduced before any other plants. Leave them about a month before introducing other plants. Examples of oxygenators are: *Elodea* sp. (although these can be too vigorous and take over the pond), starwort *Callitriche autumnalis*; milfoil *Myriophyllum* sp., hornwort *Ceratophyllum demersum*, quillwort *Isoetes lacustris*. Of these starwort is especially suitable as it continues to oxygenate throughout the year.

Surface cover

Floating leaves covering part of the water surface are vital in maintaining the health of the pond. By shading the surface, they prevent too much sunlight from entering the water. This helps to maintain clarity and suppresses the growth of filamentous weed (which is in fact an algae). For a pond of normal size and depth between half to two thirds of the surface should be shaded by floating leaves.

WATERFORD

Chose either a suitably sized water-lily, an equivalent such as water hawthorn *Aponogeton distachyos* or fringed water-lily *Nymphoides peltata*. If you chose a water-lily, select one that is suitable in leaf spread and planting depth for your pond size. Alternatively use free-floating plants such as water soldier *Stratiotes aloides* or water violet *Hottonia palustris*.

Marginal plants

Finally, you can introduce a range of marginal plants around the pond edge. There is a huge choice, so consult a specialist book. Native plants are preferable – good examples are water forget-me-not *Myosotis palustris*, marsh marigold *Caltha palustris*, flowering rush *Butomus umbellatus*, water mint *Mentha aquatica*, and various irises, although some are invasive.

Below: Marsh marigold (left) is a marginal plant with golden-yellow flowers; Yellow flag iris (right) has bright yellow flowers and large clumps of rhizomes.

Above: A common British plant, water mint has lilac coloured flowers in summer, strongly scented when crushed.

Courtship, display and territorial behaviour

From March until late June it's difficult to go out in the garden without some aspect of breeding behaviour being on show. Whether singing or displaying, or bustling about carrying nesting material or food for hungry chicks, our garden birds give ample opportunities for those interested in bird behaviour.

Above: *A male Great Tit adopts an aggressive posture, fanning its tail, to confront a territorial rival.*

Below: *The Blackcap is a summer visitor, one of Britain's more noted songsters, fluted and melodic in full song.*

Fighting for space

Many of the smaller garden songbirds are highly territorial and most of their activities are confined to this space during the breeding season. Territorial boundaries are marked out right at the beginning of the breeding season with the older, more mature and established birds having the advantage. Disputes over territories are frequent and can often result in major clashes between individual males. Fights in some species, such as Robins, can sometimes result in serious injury or even death. Younger birds, perhaps breeding for the first time will often have to squeeze into a territory that is not only small but also badly placed, perhaps with too few feeding areas. This will have a marked effect on their breeding success and will probably mean a small brood with a poor rate of chick survival.

Singing

Territorial boundaries are marked out by a number of perches from which the male bird sings. This singing also serves to attract a mate, with the louder and more vigorous songsters being the most successful. Often several individuals of the same species can be heard singing against one another; this is particularly true in early morning. However several thrush species such as the Blackbird will sing strongly in the evening, and the Song Thrush can be often be heard singing until it is getting quite dark. In well lit urban areas, Robins often sing throughout the night

Recording the position of singing birds is one means by which ornithologists can make an assessment of the number of breeding pairs present in an area. A detailed Ordnance Survey map of the study plot is used, and during a number of visits to a site, throughout the breeding season, the precise position of singing birds is marked on the map. Over a season, a cluster of observations shows the position of each territory. Using a map of your garden and those of several neighbours, it is possible to do this in a simple fashion for yourself. Singing continues most of the way through the breeding season but reaches a peak in early May when a walk in the garden very early in the morning could reveal a dozen or more species all singing at once. Tapes or CDs can be used to assist the learning of bird song. To an accomplished birdwatcher, a good ear and keen knowledge of birdsong is a key identification aid. Song varies enormously from species to species. Some, like the Great Tit or Chiffchaff, have quite simple and monotonously repeated phrases. Others, like the Robin or Blackbird, are extremely rich and complex and to a degree can vary geographically. Several songsters, notably Starlings, are great mimics and can show what other species have been around.

Pairing up

Some birds have already formed pairs during a burst of singing activity the previous autumn, and if both birds survive the winter they will often

Right: *Unobtrusive, often on the ground, the Dunnock has a complex and fascinating courtship display.*

pair up again. Most birds, however, form pairs early in the breeding season and this usually involves a male with an established territory attracting a mate by singing and carrying out some form of display. The House Sparrow will indulge in group displays at the start of the breeding season. An unpaired female will sometimes have several males all singing and displaying to her at the same time. They flutter about with raised tails and thrust out breasts trying to make the best of their smart black bibs. Many species have complex courtship displays. For example the female Dunnock shivers her wings and tail prior to mating. Several species indulge in courtship feeding, the male bird bringing morsels of food to attract a female with which he is trying to establish a bond. Once paired, the birds will continue to consolidate this bond throughout the nesting season, through mutual preening or, in some species, greeting rituals when one of the pair returns to the nest.

Left: *Robins can fight viciously in defence of their territory, and fatalities are not rare.*

Nesting and nest-boxes

Birds nest in a wide range of different places: some are ground-nesters, some use trees and shrubs, others like Sparrowhawks build a nest on a disused Crow's nest left from a previous season. A garden with several different habitats can offer locations to suit a number of bird species. Nest boxes will provide even more niches for birds.

Birds construct their nests in a variety of ways. Some nests are completely domed, like that of the Long-tailed Tit with moss, lichens and feathers held together by spiders' webs and gossamer threads. Others are cup-shaped with finely interwoven grasses and twigs. House Martins and Swallows both build cup-shaped nests made from small pieces of mud plastered together. House Martins usually build their nests colonially, underneath the eaves of houses, often in suburban streets. Swallows will nest on ledges and beams in outhouses and barns in the countryside. Artificial House Martin nests can be used successfully if a suitable location is available.

Nest boxes

A number of species will readily use a nest box if there is a shortage of natural sites. Nest box designs range from a small box for a hole-nester such as a Blue Tit, to a box large enough for a Tawny Owl, which can be slung under a branch on a large tree. The BTO produces a guide containing details of many of these and offering guidance in their construction. It is called *Nestboxes* by Chris du Feu and is available by direct mail order from the BTO.

The standard nest box can be constructed to allow the box to be opened for cleaning at the end of the season. All disturbance should be minimized, so avoid inspecting the nest box while it is being used. When a nest box is placed in the garden for the first time you need to be aware that dead nestlings and sterile eggs are commonly found in the box when it is cleaned out at the end of the year. This is a regular and natural occurrence and will happen in most seasons.

Siting of the box needs careful consideration – it must not be placed too low on a trunk otherwise the nest will become an easy target for predators such as cats, a minimum of 2 m is about right. It should face away from direct sunlight unless there are overhanging branches that offer shade. The size of the hole is species critical and should be 28 mm for Blue Tit and Great Tit. If you want to keep out the dominant Great Tit, then a Blue Tit can just squeeze in through a 25 mm hole. Nuthatches also use nest boxes and if the hole is too large they will reduce

Where House Martins are present, a muddy puddle (left) *provides the material with which to create their colonial nests of mud under the eaves of buildings* (above).

it by plastering mud round the edge. For more details on hole dimensions see the box feature below.

In addition to providing extra nesting sites by putting up nest boxes, you can assist birds by making nesting material available at the right time. Puddle a patch of mud for House Martins and Swallows, and leave out fur and hair brushings from a pet for nest linings.

Above: *Long-tailed Tits construct the most delicate nest bound to a bush with gossamer and cobwebs.*

NEST BOX DIMENSIONS

SPECIES	NEST-BOX TYPE	FLOOR SIZE (CM)
Blue Tit/Coal Tit	Hole (25mm)	15x12
Great Tit	Hole (28mm)	15x12
House Sparrow/ Nuthatch	Hole (32mm)	15x15
Starling	Hole (52mm)	15x15
Robin/Wren	Open-front	10x10
Blackbird	Shelf	20x20

Nest boxes with holes (above) attract hole-nesters such as tits, whereas open-fronted boxes (right) are suited to species such as Robins or Spotted Flycatchers.

Eggs, incubation and hatching

The size of a clutch, and sometimes of the eggs themselves, depends on the availability of food, initially for the female to produce the eggs and subsequently to raise the young birds. In some species a whole nesting season may be missed if there is insufficient food.

Above: *Conditions in a nest box are cramped: when these young chicks are close to fledging there will be very little space.*

The energy expended by a female bird in forming and laying the eggs is enormous. The number of clutches laid in a season is also dependent on the food supply. The short table opposite lists typical clutch size, incubation period and egg colour for a few garden birds. There are some clear links between size of species, number of broods, clutch size and probably longevity. Smaller birds do not have a long life expectancy and are subject to the greatest predation. Hence, to maintain the population, clutch sizes tend to be larger with more broods. The table shows that some species such as Blackbird have an extremely busy breeding season with from 3-5 broods being raised. Many garden birds lay one egg every day until the clutch is complete; larger birds have longer intervals between eggs. Several species lay coloured eggs – they tend to be species with open cup nests in need of some camouflage. Hole-nesting birds tend to lay white eggs. The Wood Pigeon has an open nest but starts to incubate as soon as the first egg is laid.

In the majority of garden birds, the females incubate the eggs. Shortly before laying, feathers are shed from a part of the breast to form a brood patch which has an especially rich blood supply. This acts as a sort of radiator for incubation and allows the sitting bird to

Right: *The eggs of Starling (right), Blackbird (left) and House Sparrow (bottom) show a variety of colour and pattern.*

Left: *Song Thrushes build an open-cupped, mud-lined nest, placed low down in thick foliage such as ivy.*

regulate the temperature of the eggs. The eggs are regularly moved and turned over to allow the whole clutch to develop. Small birds tend to wait until the clutch is complete before they start to incubate, thus ensuring that the eggs hatch within a relatively short time of each other. In some species, such as Kestrels, eggs are incubated as soon as they are laid, resulting in chicks of differing size. Survival of all raptor chicks depends on the food supply, the eldest having a distinct advantage over its younger siblings.

DETAILS OF CLUTCH AND INCUBATION FOR SOME COMMON SPECIES

SPECIES	CLUTCH SIZE	INCUBATION PERIOD	EGG COLOUR
Wood Pigeon	2, 2 broods	17 days	White
Tawny Owl	3–4, 1 brood	28–30 days	White
Swift	2–3, 1 brood	20–22 days	white
Swallow	4–5, 2–3 broods	14–15 days	White, red-spotted
Wren	5–6. 2 broods	14–15 days	White
Dunnock	4–5, 2–3 broods	14 days	Sky blue
Robin	5–6, 2 broods	14 days	White/bluish, red-spotted
Blackbird	3–5, 3–5 broods	13 days	Green-blue, freckled brown
Song Thrush	4–6, 2–3 broods	13–14 days	Blue, black spotted
Blue Tit	5–12, 1–2 broods	14 days	White, red flecks
Chaffinch	3–5, 1–2 broods	12–14 days	Blue, purple marks
House Sparrow	3–5, 2–4 broods	14 days	White, blotched brown

Feeding young and fledging

From the table below you can see, for the same 12 species, how long it takes for young to fledge and also for them to become independent. There are some interesting differences evident between the different species in the chart.

The largest bird on the list, the Tawny Owl, understandably has the longest time for fledging and also the longest period to achieve independence. This will also be a function of the time taken to acquire the necessary hunting skills. The Wood Pigeon shows a wide range of possible fledging time; this is probably linked to food availability. Young Swifts are independent as soon as they leave the nest and presumably gain their aerial insect-catching skills in large mixed flocks of birds. The smaller species all seem to take a similar time to fledge and gain independence, with the exception of the Song Thrush, which appears to take an extremely long time to fledge.

The fledging period is a time when the availability of food is very critical and it is at this time that the provision of live food such as meal worms to garden birds can be extremely beneficial. Adult birds will continue to feed themselves on the peanuts and seeds from the feeders while giving the live food to their young.

Abandoned youngsters

What do you do when you find an apparently abandoned young bird? The answer is: Leave it alone!

Its parents are probably nearby searching for food, and will continue to feed it once you have gone. Only if you are absolutely sure that it has been abandoned may you intervene. Then be prepared for a huge commitment in time and effort. The unfortunate likelihood is that you will not succeed.

FLEDGING DETAILS FOR SOME COMMON SPECIES		
SPECIES	FLEDGING TIME	INDEPENDENCE TIME
Wood Pigeon	20–35 days	1 week
Tawny Owl	32–37 days	12 weeks
Swift	5–7 weeks	On leaving nest
Swallow	19–21 days	3 weeks
Wren	16–17 days	1–3 weeks
Dunnock	12 days	2 weeks
Robin	13–14 days	3 weeks
Blackbird	13–14 days	3 weeks
Song Thrush	26–28 days	3 weeks
Blue Tit	18 days	4 weeks
Chaffinch	12–14 days	2–3 weeks
House Sparrow	15 days	1 week

Left: *In the last few days before fledging Great Spotted Woodpecker young can be very noisy when feeding.*

Above: *Bullfinches build their nest in a dense hedge, and raise at least two broods of from four to five young from late April onwards.*

Right: *The Spotted Flycatcher is an insectivorous species, but in fact nearly all small birds feed their chicks on insects to some extent. Therefore a spell of bad weather, that makes insects scarce, can affect chick development.*

Spring migration

Birdwatchers look forward eagerly to migration times. Spring migration is when summer migrants return from their winter quarters in Africa or the south Atlantic and this is a concentrated affair with the birds focused on breeding.

Most summer migrants arrive in the second half of April and early May although the very first birds, like Sand Martins or Swallows, appear in late March. This is also when many winter visitors return to continental Europe. Thrushes like Fieldfares go back to Scandinavia, Bewick's and Whooper Swans to the Arctic tundra.

In the autumn the process is reversed, summer visitors depart, winter visitors arrive and seabirds return to the Atlantic. This is also the time of year when rare vagrants turn up, it seems from almost anywhere. Small Siberian warblers appear in variable numbers on the east coast; the west coast might see the arrival of North American song birds whipped across the north Atlantic on fast moving depressions.

Below: *Most Spotted Flycatchers winter south of the equator. This is one of our latest returning migrants.*

Some of the breeding seabirds in the UK undertake the longest migrations of any bird species. An Arctic Tern, ringed at a UK breeding colony, was recovered in Australia and this species regularly winters in the pack-ice belt around Antarctica.

Migration is a complex phenomenon and raises a number of questions about why and how birds carry out such vast journeys. There is a wealth of further reading and one or two titles are listed on p124.

Local movements

Migration can also take place on a far smaller and local scale. A number of birds breed in woodland or farmland and take advantage of garden feeding stations in winter. Results from the BTO Garden Bird Survey show this seasonal variation extremely well. Other birds, such as the Snow Bunting, breed on the high tops and undertake altitudinal migrations, spending the winter on the coast.

Migrations are not undertaken only on a yearly basis; some movements might be in response to extremes of weather or due to a failure in local food supply. These can lead to irruptions in certain species; a typical example is the Waxwing, which arrives in varying numbers each winter, depending on the availability of food in its more northern breeding grounds. Cold weather movements and irruptions are dealt with in more detail in the winter section.

Passing through gardens

People observing birds in their gardens will be aware each spring of birds moving through on migration, whether they are Swallows flying overhead or a Willow Warbler staying and singing for a day. City dwellers will notice the return of the Swifts to their local colony, arriving each year at about the same date. Other species are far less consistent in their arrival times, perhaps as a result of bad weather en route. In the autumn, signs of migration are more difficult to detect for garden-based watchers but large flocks of Starlings can be seen moving to evening roosts and the sound of Redwings flying over the suburbs can be heard on quiet autumn evenings. Those with gardens sited close to the east and south coasts can sometimes wake to find their gardens full of newly arrived birds. However this is far less common in the spring when birds are pre-occupied with breeding and move on very quickly until they reach their destination.

Rarities

From time to time very scarce birds or even rarities turn up in people's gardens. To a keen birdwatcher, a rarity is a species that is sufficiently unusual that a description of the bird and the circumstances surrounding its discovery need to be submitted for vetting before they can be accepted as valid. There are bodies in each county carrying out this function and the national body is the BBRC, the 'British Birds Rarities Committee'. The likelihood of you finding a rarity in your garden is fairly small and diminishes the further your garden is from the coast. But, in some highly favoured migration hot-spots it does occur more frequently. Many gardens in villages on the North Norfolk Coast have had rare birds as visitors. There are several other coastal sites around the country that also attract scarce vagrant birds.

Apart from rarities, uncommon birds probably visit gardens in the countryside and outer suburbs more frequently than their owners realise. I have lived in my current house in Barnet, North London, for only two years but during that time I have seen a number of spring and autumn migrants in or from the garden. Initial identification of a number of these was by having a reasonable knowledge of bird song. Others, such as Hobby, I have seen by being in the garden and looking up at the right time.

Above: *Rarities do occur! Hoopoes very occasionally turn up in country gardens.*

Below: *The Lesser Whitethroat is a summer visitor. It takes an easterly route to winter quarters in arid sub-Saharan Africa.*

Predators and pests

There are a number of predators of garden birds. The level of threat depends on the time of year and the location. However, irrespective of where the garden is and in all seasons, the domestic cat is the most significant predator.

If cats are frequent visitors to your garden, this threat can be reduced by the careful siting of your feeders and nest boxes. Access can be made more difficult with dense prickly hedges such as Holly and by discouraging cats from lingering around feeding stations. If you have a cat then keep it well fed and try to keep it in at key times like early morning and dusk and during the breeding season. A bell placed on a collar around the cat's neck is an effective deterrent. Unless you specifically want to breed the cats, they should be neutered, which will help to keep down the feral population. The scale of the potential predation can be gauged from the fact that there are in excess of seven million domestic cats in the UK. Up to one in three of them lives in a feral state, i.e. in the wild. Feral cats take proportionally more birds than cats fed at home as pets. There is a wide range of estimates for the number of birds killed by cats in the UK, ranging from 30 to 75 million per year.

The grey squirrel is a lesser threat, mainly in the breeding season when nest boxes will be attacked, the holes enlarged and eggs and nestlings taken.

Raptors represent a more natural enemy to garden birds and both Sparrowhawks and Kestrels will often raid garden feeding stations. Kestrels are more of a threat in suburban and inner city areas. Here birds such as House Sparrows form a greater part of their diet than in the country, where more rodents are taken.

Other avian pests are various members of the crow family, chiefly Carrion Crow and Magpie, both of which rob nests and are a threat in the breeding season.

Above: *Studies show that increased Magpie numbers have not greatly affected garden bird breeding.*

Below: *There is no more effective and ruthless predator of garden birds than the domestic cat.*

Key spring species

In early spring the last of the winter visiting species such as Fieldfare, Redwing and Brambling leave for their northern breeding grounds. In their place a continuous stream of summer visitors arrive from the south. The earliest such as Sand Martins and Wheatears start to arrive early in March, whereas Spotted Flycatchers will not arrive until later in May. Some of these birds have come from southern Europe. Others from much further, many from south of the Sahara. They have all arrived to breed.

GREY HERON *Ardea cinerea*
Length 90–100cm (36–40in)

Resident. A very large, long-legged wading bird with grey, white and black plumage

Unless you have a pond in your garden all you are likely to see of a Grey Heron is a view of one flapping overhead on its way to a nearby lake. If you have a pond, however, it is quite possible that you or rather your goldfish have been the victim of a dawn raid from this bird. Grey Herons nest in colonies and can be found not only in the country but also in the middle of large cities. There is a breeding colony of about twenty-

Above: *Herons look out of place on their treetop nests.*

five pairs on an island in a lake in Regent's Park, London. Nests consist of a large and untidy bundle of sticks and are most frequently situated high up in groups of large trees, although reedbeds and cliffs are also sometimes used. Breeding takes place early in the year, with most eggs being laid by the end of March. Grey Herons eat a wide variety of aquatic life including fish, amphibians, insects and small mammals, changing to suit seasonal availability. The species is fairly evenly distributed throughout the UK both in the breeding season and in winter and has steadily increased its population in Europe during the 20th century.

Left: *Herons are frequent early morning visitors to quiet gardens, in search of frogs and goldfish.*

SPARROWHAWK *Accipiter nisus*
Length: 28–38cm (11–15in)

Resident. A small grey and brown bird of prey, with blunt rounded wings and a long tail.

The Sparrowhawk is a bird of woodlands, hedgerows and mature gardens, usually seen dashing at high speed in agile pursuit of small birds, which are its main prey item. It was one of the species that crashed in numbers in the 1950s and '60s owing to the effects of pesticides such as DDT and dieldrin. Since then, the population has recovered and birds are once again being seen throughout the UK, including city suburbs with mature gardens. They are generally secretive birds, although in the early spring they are probably at their most visible, indulging in spectacular soaring and slow-flapping display

flights over their nest site. In winter, when garden feeding stations are at their busiest, Sparrowhawks will use them as a food source, approaching the bird table in a rapid level flight often weaving in and out of bushes and trees before snatching a small bird in mid-air. Prey is usually taken to a nearby perch, where it will be plucked before being eaten. The nest is built in a bush or tree and is loosely constructed from twigs. Three to six bluish-white brown-blotched eggs are incubated for four or five weeks. The chicks fledge after a further three to four weeks in the nest. Immediately prior to fledging, the young birds can be quite noisy and it is at this time that nests may be discovered.

Above: *Mid-morning on a fine, still, early spring day is the best time to look for displaying Sparrowhawks. They can be seen soaring and diving over woodland and copses in the area of their breeding territory.*

Left: *Sparrowhawks feed almost exclusively on other birds. The female is usually much larger than the male (shown here) and can take prey as large as a Wood Pigeon.*

TURTLE DOVE *Streptopelia turtur*
Length: 26–29cm (10–11in)

Spring/Summer visitor. A small dove, slim with a long tail and grey, rufous-brown and black plumage with a pinkish flush to the breast.

A bird of the countryside, preferring agricultural areas with scattered open woodland and small clumps of trees, this species will only be found in or near gardens in rural areas. In the UK, its distribution is predominantly eastern and south-eastern England, extending to Yorkshire, the West Midlands and Somerset. Turtle Doves winter in Africa and are subject to heavy persecution by hunting on migration through the Mediterranean and southern Europe. They arrive in late April. These birds are relatively secretive breeders; nesting usually in scrub or deciduous woodland with the majority of nests being in elder or hawthorn.

The species is mostly known for its characteristic and very distinctive soft purring call. They are ground feeders on plant and grass seeds and are often seen out in the middle of fields or meadows. Return migration is mainly in September and in both spring and autumn there is a passage of continental birds on the east coast.

Above: *The Turtle Dove is subject to heavy hunting pressure in the Mediterranean countries as it migrates northwards to its breeding grounds.*

Above: *In flight the turtle dove shows a distinctive white rim to its tail.*

Left: *Turtle Doves feed on the ground and early in the morning they can be seen at the roadside picking up grit, which helps digestion.*

CUCKOO *Cuculus canorus*
Length: 32–34cm (13–14in)

Spring/Summer visitor. Long-tailed with pointed wings, predominantly grey with a small proportion of females a rufous-brown. Familiar and universally known two-note song.

The Cuckoo occurs fairly commonly in most types of open countryside with scattered bushes and trees, especially large marshlands and heaths. Its shape is similar to a small falcon or hawk but it has a distinctive direct flight with shallow wingbeats, coloration and the pointed wings distinguishing it from Kestrel and Sparrowhawk. It is widespread throughout Britain and Ireland but at its most common in south and central England, although there is evidence of a decline in the population. As a visitor to gardens it will only be known in more rural areas and then

Left: The flight silhouette is distinctive, with pointed wings and a long tail.

mainly from its song. It arrives during April and early May. It is unique among British birds with its breeding habit of parasitism on other birds and laying its eggs in the nests of host species. Resident species receive eggs first followed by summer migrants as they arrive and start breeding. Various species are targeted, depending on habitat and local abundance. Egg-laying is timed to ensure that the cuckoo egg hatches first. The young cuckoo soon ejects the other eggs and any other nestlings from the nest, leaving the host parents to raise a chick often several times their size. The male cuckoo's song is very familiar and heard incessantly during May and June. The females have a bubbling call. Return passage to tropical Africa is from the end of July to early September.

Above: The Cuckoo lays a single egg in a host's nest, the colour of the shell often imitating that of the host's egg.

Left: The young cuckoo reaches a stage where it is far larger than the adult hosts.

GREEN WOODPECKER *Picus viridis*
Length: 30–33cm (11½–13in)

Resident. A green Jackdaw-sized bird with black face and bright red crown, yellow rump noticeable in flight.

The Green Woodpecker, with its distinctive plumage and call, is one of our most conspicuous woodland and heathland birds. It has a widespread distribution in England except for upland areas. In Scotland it is confined mainly to the south-east and in Ireland it is unknown. Although it is found in deciduous and mixed woodland, it is equally a bird of parkland, heaths, large mature gardens and well-timbered cultivated land.

Above: The yellow rump is striking in undulating flight, wings folded shut between bursts of wingbeats.

Below: Green Woodpeckers feed mainly on ants taken from anthills in mature grassland.

Its call is a far-reaching, powerful laughing 'klu' repeated rapidly 6–8 times and is heard most frequently in the early morning and in spring. It has spread quite noticeably in suburban green spaces in recent years. This is chiefly due to the reduction in regular mowing of grassland. There has been a consequent increase in invertebrates and especially ants. It is a specialist feeder on ants and is often seen on the ground energetically excavating a large anthill. Breeding takes place over a long period and eggs may be laid at any time from mid-March to the end of June, nest holes being sited in the main trunk of a mature tree several metres above the ground. Juveniles are easily distinguished from adults with streaking on the breast and a generally more scaly appearance. Green Woodpeckers tend to be quite sedentary, not wandering far from the breeding area even in the winter.

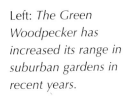

Left: The Green Woodpecker has increased its range in suburban gardens in recent years.

GREAT SPOTTED WOODPECKER *Dendrocopos major*
Length: 22–24cm (8½–9½in)

Resident. A striking black and white blackbird-sized bird with an undulating flight.

The Great Spotted Woodpecker is widespread throughout England and Scotland, wherever there are trees and is the commonest woodpecker in Britain, found in woodlands, parks and gardens. It is not found on the higher upland areas and is not present at all in Ireland. This species is the most frequently seen of the British woodpeckers and is usually fairly vocal, the presence of the bird often being given away by its distinctive 'tschick' call and also by the sound of its far-carrying and very rapid drumming. The drum of the Great Spotted Woodpecker is by far the fastest of the European woodpeckers at 10–15 strikes per second. In the UK it is easily distinguished from other species by either size or coloration. Both sexes share the black and white plumage and have a reddish pink vent but the female lacks the male's bright red nape patch. The juvenile has a completely red crown and a paler pink vent. The main food is a range of insects and larvae found under bark and in decaying

The male Great Spotted Woodpecker (right) has a red nape, which is lacking in female (above).

timber. In the winter a variety of foods are taken from feeding stations, especially peanuts. A mixture of crushed peanut, seeds and fat wedged into crevices in the bark of a tree is also attractive to this species.

Great Spotted Woodpeckers are also known to feed on the eggs and young of other birds and to bore their way into nest boxes to get at the contents. The nest hole is found at varying heights, from 2–8 m high on the main trunk of trees, often taking advantage of dead or dying timber. For a few days before fledging the young birds are often very noisy and then nests are relatively easy to locate.

Left: *The Great Spotted Woodpecker has white spots on its wings and patches on its shoulders that stand out in flight.*

BARN SWALLOW *Hirundo rustica*
Length: 16–22cm (6½–8½in)

Spring/Summer visitor. Unmistakable small aerial bird with dark upperparts, creamy white breast and very long tail streamers.

The Barn Swallow arrives from its African wintering grounds between the end of March and through to mid May. The species is widespread throughout Britain and Ireland and in the BTO *Atlas of Breeding Birds* it is recorded in virtually every 10-km square. The population declined by some 15% in the late 20th century, primarily as a result of changing agricultural practices which both reduced nest sites and the numbers of flying insects. However, since 1994 numbers have been increasing with a rise of 25%. The Swallow is common in cultivated country with villages and farms; it is not found in larger towns and cities and will only be seen in these areas when flying through on migration. During migration Swallows often congregate in very large numbers over wetlands and lakes owing to the concentration of airborne

Above: *In spring the long tail streamers create a distinctive appearance.*

insects on which they feed exclusively. At these times, they will often roost in flocks in reedbeds. Return migration is over an extended period and lasts from August until well into October. The commonest call is a twittering 'vit' 'vit' and other calls are used to warn of the presence of aerial predators such as the Hobby. The nest is a half-cup made of mud and is placed on beams in outbuildings and barns or in recesses in buildings. The availability of flying insects has a major impact on breeding success, and widespread and prolonged cold wet weather causes seasonal swings in cal and national populations.

Above: *Natural nest sites have been almost entirely replaced by ledges in outbuildings, such as barns and stables.*

Right: *Swallows often gather on overhead wires in late summer and autumn, prior to starting their journey to South Africa.*

HOUSE MARTIN *Delichon urbica*
Length: 12–13cm (4½–5in)

Spring/Summer visitor. Small, compact bird with dark upperparts and a white rump. Throat, breast and belly are also white.

House Martins are common throughout Europe but are local on exposed northern and western coasts. They eat airborne insects and generally feed at a greater height than Swallows, concentrating on smaller, higher flying insects. In some ways the House Martin has more in common with the Swift than the Swallow, for its choice of food is closer to the preference of the Swift and it also has the ability to nest in towns and city suburbs. House Martins winter in tropical Africa and return to the UK in April/May: Return dates can vary greatly from year to year depending on the weather en route.

Autumn migration takes place from August to October although in the UK stragglers can be seen up to December and very occasionally January. The call is a clear high 'prrit' and this often gives away the bird's presence. This species breeds in colonies. The nests consist of almost fully enclosed mud cups usually placed under the eaves of buildings, although colonies are also found away from towns on cliff faces.

Provision of a muddy puddle in a garden will often encourage visits from nest-building birds if there is a colony in the area. Large flocks of House Martins often gather over water on migration, especially in the autumn and these concentrations of birds often attract predators such as Hobbies.

Above: *Artificial nests correctly placed under the eaves can encourage House Martins to colonize a building.*

Left: *House Martins usually catch high-flying insects, but can be seen over suburban houses and gardens.*

Above: *Clean white under-parts and rump help identification in mixed flocks of hirundines.*

DUNNOCK *Prunella modularis*
Length: 14–15cm (5½–6in)

Resident. A small unobtrusive bird with a dark appearance, a grey breast and subtly marked with brown and black on the upperparts.

This is a common garden bird that often goes unnoticed owing to its liking for dense shrubbery. This is especially true during the breeding season when the nest is usually approached through thick cover. The song is fairly distinctive and consists of a jumble of short trills and a squeaky high warble; this is delivered throughout the male's territory often from a low shrub in the early morning. The call is a loud and shrill 'seeeeee'. In Britain, the Dunnock breeds in suburban parks and gardens and in the country in scrub and hedgerows on farmland. Breeding behaviour is complex, with displays by the female involving wing shivering and tail quivering prior to mating. In the breeding season and the autumn it is mainly insectivorous, switching to a diet

Above: *In the winter Dunnocks venture out from the shelter of shrubs to forage for seeds on the ground.*

that also includes small seeds in the winter, mainly taken while foraging on the ground. In the UK, it is mainly sedentary, with the population being augmented by visitors from northern Europe which are present from September until March/April. The Dunnock is found throughout Britain and Ireland but is fairly sparse in the Scottish highlands and on the Hebrides. A recently published report produced by the BTO and the RSPB records a decline of just over 25% in the Dunnock's UK population comparing 2006 to 1970. A major contributor to this has been changing agricultural practices, in particular those causing the loss of hedgerows.

Left: *Unobtrusive habits mean that the Dunnock often goes unnoticed in gardens.*

SONG THRUSH *Turdus philomelos*
Length: 22–24cm (8½–9½in)

Resident. A typical thrush with earthy grey-brown upperparts and strongly spotted beneath.

The Song Thrush population in the UK had declined by 50% in 2006 compared with the level in 1970. This is due to changing farming practice, particularly in arable land where chick production and survival are a problem because of lack of food. Gardens are therefore becoming especially important for this species, and those gardens where chemicals are not used extensively and hence insects are in abundance have become valuable habitats. Song Thrushes eat mainly worms, snails and insects, with fruits and berries in the autumn. Snail shells are often found in abundance next to a stone that is used as an anvil to assist in their smashing. The Song Thrush is a notable songster with a varied mixture of soft fluted notes and harsher phrases repeated three or four times followed by a short pause before a different theme takes over. Its song is most noticeable at dusk. In this country, it is common in parks and gardens, where it is often seen feeding on open lawns and foraging along the edges through the leaf litter. It is also fairly common in woodland and in hedgerows. In the 1988–1991 Breeding Bird Survey this species was found in virtually every 10-km square in the UK and was missing from only the most open areas. The population increases from September until April with the addition of birds from northern and central Europe.

Right: *The Song Thrush shows a browny-orange flash under the wing in flight.*

Below: *Song Thrushes are one of only a few birds to use a tool – they break open snail shells by hitting them against a stone.*

Above: *The Song Thrush has one of the most varied and melodious songs of any garden bird.*

GARDEN WARBLER *Sylvia borin*
Length: 13–15cm (5–6in)

Spring/Summer visitor. A small grey-buff bird with no contrasting features, darker upperparts and a dark eye.

The Garden Warbler is a long-distance migrant wintering in southern and central Africa and some way south of the drought-prone Sahel region. In spring, it arrives mainly in May although some appear in late April. As a garden bird, this species will mainly be known in mature gardens sited in rural areas and adjacent to deciduous woodland or scrub with dense ground cover. It has a rich and varied song, delivered

Right: *The Garden Warbler is one of the UK's best songsters, with a similar song to that of the Blackcap.*

often from a perch in deep cover, which is similar to that of the Blackcap but without the higher fluted notes of that species. Like most warblers, it is insectivorous during most of the season in the UK, adding berries to its diet later in the year. It is often difficult to see and spends much time skulking in dense undergrowth. The nest is placed on or close to the ground in very dense cover. In the UK it is fairly common except in northern Scotland and in uplands or fen country lacking suitable habitat.

It is almost entirely absent from much of Ireland. In the mid 1970s there was a dip in the population caused by its passage through the drought-stricken Sahel region to the south of the Sahara.

Above: *Young Garden Warblers are fed almost exclusively on insects.*

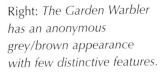

Right: *The Garden Warbler has an anonymous grey/brown appearance with few distinctive features.*

COMMON WHITETHROAT *Sylvia communis*
Length: 13–14cm (5–6in)

Spring/Summer visitor. A small active and noisy scrub warbler, grey on crown and back, rufous-brown on wings. Underparts buff tinged pink on spring male.

The Whitethroat may be seen in or near mature gardens situated in the outer suburbs and in rural areas. It favours sunny sites of scrub and weedy thickets, hedgerows and woodland edges. It is an active bird often heard issuing a variety of alarm calls from within bushes, It has a busy, scratchy warbling song, which is either delivered from a perch on the top of a bush or in a parachuting display flight. The nest is placed low in thick bushes and four or five off-white eggs with dark spots are incubated for twelve to fourteen days before hatching. Fledging takes place after a further eleven or twelve days. Whitethroats return on spring migration in April–May and leave during August–September with stragglers into October. The favoured wintering area is in the drought-prone Sahel region south of the Sahara Desert in Africa. In 1969 three-quarters of the UK Whitethroat population failed to reappear in the spring owing to droughts in the Sahel. Numbers continued to decline and reached a low point in 1974. A slow recovery in numbers of returning birds was followed by further crashes in 1983/84 and in 1991. The recent RSPB and BTO publication *The State of the UK's Birds in 2007* shows the recent population at a level 31% higher than in 1970. This is still far lower than the level prior to the 1969 crash. Currently Whitethroats occur throughout England and Wales but with a much patchier distribution in Scotland and Ireland.

Right: *For the most part Whitethroats feed on insects, although in the autumn berries are eaten as well.*

Above: *The Whitethroat often sings during the 'parachuting' display flight between song perches.*

CHIFFCHAFF *Phylloscopus collybita*
Length: 10–12cm (4–4¾in)

Spring/Summer visitor. Small numbers overwinter in sheltered locations. Small grey-green warbler, dark legs. Similar to Willow Warbler but with very different song.

The Chiffchaff is widespread throughout England, Wales and Ireland, although it is far less common in the north of England, and sparse in Scotland. It is mainly restricted in the breeding season to areas having fairly tall deciduous trees and it only frequents conifers if there are deciduous trees nearby. Its presence in the spring is usually given away by its monotonous two-syllable song. In gardens it is known chiefly in rural areas or in suburban fringes having mature gardens adjacent to large trees. The majority of Chiffchaffs winter around the Mediterranean and in tropical Africa. They are among our earliest spring migrants, returning to the UK from late March onwards. Autumn migration is protracted and runs from August through into November. It is complicated by the arrival in autumn of Chiffchaffs from northern and eastern races, some of which overwinter along with a few UK breeding birds. In winter chiffchaffs prefer lower, scrubbier vegetation, in particular sallow bushes. Like other related warblers they mostly feed on insects and are adept at flycatching.

The Chiffchaff is named after its song, a much repeated two note whistle, the first note being higher.

The Chiffchaff (above) is slightly smaller than Willow Warbler (left) with dark legs. The different songs are the easiest way to separate them.

SPOTTED FLYCATCHER *Muscicapa striata*
Length: 13.5–15cm (5½–6in)

Spring/Summer visitor. Dull grey-brown with off-white underparts streaked dark brown. Crown is also streaked.

Spotted Flycatchers are found throughout Britain and Ireland although rather more sparsely in the north and west. The recent RSPB-BTO study shows a very significant drop in numbers over recent years, with 85% less in 2006 than in 1970. This reflects a general decline in those species associated with woodlands. Spotted Flycatchers prefer open woodland and woodland edge, including open pine forest but they are also found in parks and gardens, where they can breed in close proximity to people. Their characteristic feeding strategy is to sit upright on an exposed twig, branch or fence-post and then to sally out in pursuit of flying insects. It uses a wide range of nesting locations including niches on damaged trees and buildings, and open-fronted nest boxes. The main call is a thin scratchy 'tseeeeeh' usually delivered from an exposed perch. It has a very insignificant song consisting of call-like squeaks repeated three or four times. They are one of the latest western European migrants to arrive, with the bulk of birds turning up in May. Return passage is mostly in September.

Above: *Spotted Flycatchers perch on a branch or a post when flycatching, from where they will dart out to catch a passing crane fly or butterfly.*

Below: *Spotted Flycatchers often favour the same perch, to which they habitually return. They prefer open-fronted nest boxes, and often nest close to buildings – or even inside them (left).*

LONG-TAILED TIT *Aegithalos caudatus*
Length: 12–14cm (5–6in)

Resident. Tiny birds, black above and white beneath with pinkish-brown backs. Tail longer than body.

The Long-tailed Tit is widespread throughout the British Isles but is significantly more common in the south and east; density reduces greatly to the north and west, especially in urban areas and in uplands. The recent BTO/RSPB study shows that the population has increased significantly by about 49% over the past forty years. It is a bird of bushy mixed or deciduous scrub and woodland with a distinct liking for areas of wet woodland close to streams and lakes. It is quite common in mature suburban gardens where there is an appreciable stretch of linked trees and shrubs. In the autumn and in winter Long-tailed Tits are highly gregarious and move through the woods and gardens in small mixed groups with other tit species and goldcrests. They are fairly noisy when in these roaming parties and an approaching group is often given away by the distinctive noises of the flock. The commonest call is a short purring 'tser-rr' and also a 'tek'-like clicking call. They feed mainly on small insects and invertebrates. The population level can drop enormously during a severe winter when access to such foods is limited. After a particularly hard winter, like 1962/63 it may take several seasons to recover. Nest building starts fairly early in the season, sometimes in early March in the south of England. The nest is a fairly large oval domed construction with a side entrance and is made from woven feathers and cobwebs, usually disguised with lichens. It is sited in a dense bush or tree, close to the trunk and sometimes several metres above the ground. The clutch size varies from six to twelve eggs and incubation takes about fifteen days.

Above: *The tail makes up over half of a Long-tailed Tit's overall length.*

Below: *Young Long-tailed Tits have shorter tails than adults and are darker round the face, head and nape.*

BLUE TIT *Parus caeruleus*
Length: 11–12cm (4½–5in)

Resident. Small, predominantly yellow and blue with a distinctive black and white head pattern.

The Blue Tit is common throughout the UK and Ireland and is missing only from upland areas, the Northern Isles and is very sparse on the Hebrides. It is a highly regular visitor to suburban gardens, especially feeders and bird tables and it frequently makes use of nest-boxes when provided. Its preferred habitat however is oak woodland, where the population reaches its highest densities. There is a large overlap in the nesting and food requirements of Blue and Great Tits and, where they compete, Great Tits dominate. In common with other tit species and small birds such as treecreepers, Goldcrests and Long-tailed Tits, Blue Tits form mixed flocks. In autumn and winter these flocks can be seen roaming though the woods and gardens foraging for food. Blue Tits have a very wide range of calls, especially a repeated 'churr, churr, churr'. Food consists of small insects and larvae and, to a lesser extent, seeds and berries. The breeding is timed to coincide with the emergence of small caterpillars, which are available in countless numbers every spring in oak woods. The Blue Tit lays one of the largest clutches of all British bird species, commonly ranging from eight to twelve eggs and not infrequently up to fifteen or sixteen.

Incubation is short as in most small birds and lasts twelve to fourteen days and the young birds fledge and leave the nest after a further three weeks. Double broods are extremely uncommon. Blue Tits are frequent users of nest boxes and are prone to predation by squirrels and occasionally woodpeckers, which reach the eggs or chicks by enlarging the entrance hole. This can be protected by placing a steel plate with a suitably sized hole over the existing entrance. The hole-size is critical and a hole of 25 mm will prevent use by Great Tits and sparrows where there is competition for nest space.

Above: *In the past, Blue Tits have been notorious for opening foil caps on milk bottles and stealing cream.*

Below: *Blue Tit sexes are very similar, although the female is usually a little duller.*

Below: *Blue Tits take readily to nest boxes in gardens, the small hole excludes larger species.*

GREAT TIT *Parus major*
Length: 13.5–14.5cm (5½in)

Resident. Small bird with boldly marked black and white head, breast yellow with black centre. Back green with blue wings fringed white.

The Great Tit along with the Blue Tit is among the commonest visitors to gardens both in the town and the country. Its chief habitat is open deciduous woodland, but it can be found just about anywhere there are a few shrubs and trees and is also found in conifer plantations. It has a very familiar song with a frequently repeated 'teacher, teacher' phrase which can be heard on warm days from the middle of the winter right through to its normal nesting month

of May. The distribution map shows that it is widespread throughout the UK and Ireland except in the uplands and the more exposed northern and western islands. It depends on seeds to a far greater extent than the Blue Tit, especially on beech. The population rises and falls in line with the size of the beech crop. Great Tits, like Blue Tits, are hole-nesters and this is the main factor determining the location of the nest site. The species readily takes to using nest boxes. However, mature oak woods are preferred and in less favourable habitats for nest holes, such as hedgerows and scrub, breeding numbers are lower. Clutch size ranges from five to eleven eggs, but with a tendency to smaller clutches in less than optimum habitats. Incubation and fledging periods are similar to those for the Blue Tit at twelve to fourteen days and twenty days respectively. The BTO/RSPB study shows that the Great Tit population has increased by about 90% in the past forty years.

Above: *Like most of their relatives, Great Tits are highly acrobatic feeders.*

Above: *Great Tits hunt through foliage for insects.*

Left: *The female Great Tit* (above) *is duller than the male* (below), *with a narrower black breast and belly stripe.*

JACKDAW *Corvus monedula*
Length: 32–34cm (12½–13½in)

Resident and partial migrant. Small dark crow with grey nape and pale eye. Skilful flyer and fairly vocal.

In the larger cities the Jackdaw is a bird of the suburban fringe and will regularly visit gardens in these areas. It is also found commonly in towns and villages where it nests colonially in older trees offering nest holes and on old buildings such as church towers. The species is found throughout the UK and Ireland but is largely absent from the west and north-west of Scotland. Jackdaws are gregarious birds and are often seen in tumbling acrobatic flight around tall buildings and on the coast around sea-cliffs. The most common call is a metallic 'chek' which once learnt is extremely distinctive. Jackdaws feed mainly on the invertebrates found on or close to the surface of fields and especially grazed grassland. They are at their most abundant in those areas where the grazing of sheep and cattle is still common. Nests are built of sticks and are to be found in holes in old trees, crevices and holes in buildings and in similar locations on natural crags and sea-cliffs. The species is a partial migrant and northern and eastern populations move eastwards into western Europe to spend the winter.

Above (top): *Jackdaws are very gregarious, forming noisy agile flocks, particularly at evening roosts.*

Above (bottom): *In rural areas Jackdaws favour trees with suitable nest holes as breeding sites.*

Left: *Town Jackdaws like older buildings with crevices and ledges.*

GREENFINCH *Carduelis chloris*
Length: 14–15cm (5½–6in)

Resident with some winter movements. A large, chunky, yellow-green finch with a strong bill.

This species is the most abundant and also the largest of the yellow-green finches and is widely found in parks and gardens. It is a regular visitor to winter feeding stations taking peanuts and seeds such as sunflower both from feeders and loose fed on bird tables and the ground. Its powerful bill allows it to feed on a wide range of naturally occurring seeds. It can be found over most of the British Isles, being absent only from treeless uplands and coastal areas in the northwest of Scotland. It is at its most common in farmland and around small towns and villages, although in response to changing agricultural practices over the past fifty years it has come to depend more on feeding in gardens and on feeding stations. Breeding takes place over a prolonged period with clutches being laid any time from April to August, some pairs raising several broods in a single season. The clutch size varies from three to six eggs and the nest is placed in a fork close to the trunk of a small tree or dense bush, often in conifers. There are some winter movements of birds, with a small proportion of UK birds moving south and west and with a compensating influx of birds from the near continent.

Left: The male Greenfinch (above) has smart green, yellow and black plumage; the female (below) is much duller.

Right: The Greenfinch is the most frequent garden visitor of the finch family.

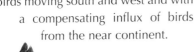

Above: Male (below) and female (above) Greenfinch both show greenish rump and yellow outer-tail feathers when flying.

Summer

Summer sees the end of the frantic activity of the breeding season, and after a seemingly brief respite, the movements of the autumn migration get underway.

For a gardener, the summer is a time to enjoy the benefit of all the hard work put in during the rest of the year. It's a time for relaxing in a deckchair, cooking barbecues and eating outdoors. At the start of the summer, birds in the garden are still in the middle of the frenetic activity of breeding. Newly fledged youngsters are everywhere facing the dangers of garden predators such as cats, magpies and crows. By the end of the summer, the situation is very different. The majority of birds have finished breeding and the garden becomes a far quieter place. Most birds cease to sing and many garden species depart for nearby fields and parks where there is an abundance of natural foods. Consumption of food from feeders and bird tables is low, but fresh water is still essential. Migration is in full swing; in my area on the outskirts of North London the local Swifts leave at the beginning of August. For high arctic breeders such as waders migration starts as early as the beginning of July. By the end of August many bird species are on the move, as their migrations steadily gather momentum, reaching a peak in autumn.

Above: The hyperactive little Wren has, for its size, one of the loudest of all songs. Right: High summer means the end of the breeding season for most birds. However Collared Doves can breed any time from February to October.

Feeding garden birds

With the start of summer, the frenetic activity of spring and the peak of the breeding season is past, although multi-brooded species are still rearing young and will continue to do so throughout the summer.

There is a wealth of natural food available – insects are especially important for feeding young birds during their fledging period, and by the end of the summer the first seeds and fruits, such as blackberries will become available. If your plant selection for your 'bird garden' has been good then you will see birds feeding on natural foods in your own garden. Plants can be chosen not only for their seeds and fruit but also for the insects that they might attract. The bird-friendly planting can be assisted if an organic regime is used to further encourage insects.

In the past, controversy has raged about the subject of artificial feeding in gardens in summer. These days it is fairly widely accepted that summer feeding is a useful supplement to the natural food that is readily available. In the past thirty years there has been a dramatic reduction in numbers of some of our farmland birds, some of which have switched to gar-

dens, both suburban and rural. There is some evidence that birds encouraged to stay and breed in gardens have lower levels of breeding success, so for some species artificial feeding can be important.

Migration is in full swing by end of August and even casual garden observers will notice the absence of the local Swifts. Large flocks of Starlings will be out and about foraging and swirling around prior to roosting. The late summer/autumn migration is a complex and protracted affair, lasting from July until October or November.

Above: *Young birds, like this Robin, are at their most vulnerable just after leaving the nest.*

Left: *In dry weather worms burrow deeper and are difficult for Blackbirds to find.*

Bird tables and loose feeding

Many bird species feed fledglings in the nest entirely on insects and other invertebrates. However, the adults may continue to take more easily available food from feeders and bird tables.

Early summer is perhaps the time when providing live food on the bird table is most useful. Mealworms can be bought at pet shops and reared at home in a suitable container filled with layers of biscuit, bran and dried bread, kept just moist with holes for aeration. Live food should be placed in a container that has a smooth inside surface to stop the mealworms etc. from escaping and which has sides sufficiently low to allow the birds secure access to the food. The container can then be sited on the bird-table, or on the ground, where it will be visited by a wide range of bird species. In a dry summer many of the birds that feed on the ground and forage for worms, insects and invertebrates have difficulty finding enough food to feed their young. If water usage regulations permit, then a part of your lawn – preferably in the shade – should be kept moist; this will allow earthworms to stay nearer the surface, making them more easily available to feeding thrushes. High-energy seed mixes formulated especially for these species will also help.

At the end of the summer seeds and fruit become abundant and garden feeding can be reduced. Natural food sources will be sufficient. If you still want the birds to visit your garden then feeding should be maintained, but don't be surprised if some species go missing for a few weeks or even a month or two as they exploit natural food sources elsewhere. The end of the summer is a relatively slack period in the year's feeding timetable and now is an ideal time to clean and disinfect feeders and repair any damage done to feeders by squirrels. The companies specialising in garden bird food and feeders send out new catalogues at this time of the year so new feeders and bulk supplies of feed can be ordered for the season to come. Names and addresses of garden bird food specialists can be found on page 124.

Above: *Providing live food can be invaluable for parent birds feeding their young in the nest.*

Below: *Large concentrations of insects attract flocks of House Martins preparing for migration.*

Feeders and other food

Feeders can be filled with high energy seed formulations. These are especially useful during the breeding season and in dry summers. At this time in particular whole peanuts must not be loose fed as they can choke young chicks. Instead, provide peanuts in feeders or in crushed form when included in loose feed. Towards the end of the summer the use of feeders can be reduced as more and more natural food becomes available.

The studies carried out by the BTO using data supplied by contributors to the Garden BirdWatch Survey show a marked seasonal variation in the records of birds in gardens. For example, in early summer, Great Spotted Woodpeckers visit gardens with young birds to show them how to use feeders, but in late summer woodland provides plenty of natural food. House Sparrow, Starling Chaffinch, Greenfinch, Goldfinch and Bullfinch are examples of regularly occurring birds that show a marked reduction in garden visiting in late summer and into the autumn. This is a national phenomenon, although in some areas, such as city centres this effect may be less marked.

The return of these birds in numbers to the garden feeding stations will in most cases not occur until the weather shows the first signs of the onset of winter. The members of the tit family are the earliest to return in numbers and attendance by Blue Tits in gardens is more regular following the trend for increased summer feeding.

Above: *Swarms of flying ants in hot weather attract opportunistic feeders such as Starlings or even Black-headed Gulls.*

Left: *High-energy seed formulations help garden birds to supplement their natural diet and breed more successfully.*

Water in the garden

The birds in your garden need a good supply of water throughout the summer months. The most obvious use is for drinking but regular bathing is essential for good feather maintenance and the additional load caused by freshly fledged young means that in the summer months water is used up quickly and becomes dirty.

Birds need water not only for feather maintenance and washing, but also for drinking – which often takes place just after feeding. So it's easy to imagine how, after a hot summer's day, the clean water that you put out earlier has become soiled with dust and feather parasites, plus food washed off in the process of preening and drinking. It is therefore essential to refill bird baths on a daily basis, rinsing them out at the same time and occasionally cleaning them with disinfectant. In very hot periods you may find the birds using the water to help them cool down. During prolonged periods without rain, it is a good idea to provide extra sources of water; containers such as plant pot trays and inverted plastic lids from old dustbins can make good instant bird baths.

Above: *Summer supplies of water are vital for drinking and bathing.*

A frequently used bird bath can give an ideal opportunity for observing birds and the interactions between species. The bird bath should be placed so that you can observe without disturbing the birds, so binoculars can come in handy if a close location is not suitable. Remember to place the bird bath in a spot where the approach of a cat can be easily noticed – an energetic bath can distract a bird's attention.

An alternative to a water-filled bird bath is provided by a dust-bath, which will be especially popular with House Sparrows. If there is a spare plastic dustbin lid it can be sunk into the soil upside down in a suitably sheltered location which is not too far from some cover. It should be filled with fine sand and earth to a depth of 5 cm. Any bath, whether for water or dust bathing, needs to be cleaned and disinfected occasionally to prevent avian diseases. The contents of the dust bath should be disposed of at regular intervals and replaced. When disinfectants are used the baths must be thoroughly rinsed in clean water to remove any trace of chemicals.

Below: *Garden pools need a shallow end to give small birds easy access.*

Ponds

By early summer the floating and marginal plants should be fully developed and your pond will have become a haven for a wide range of wildlife. If the pond has been constructed with a shallow section, birds will be frequent visitors to bathe and drink. A natural pond edge has wet margins that are home to insects and invertebrates, providing more easily accessible food for birds during dry weather. There may be tiny frogs and perhaps newts, as well as adult frogs resting in the surface layers or hidden in small iris beds.

Water invertebrates are quick to colonize – waterboatmen, whirly-gig beetles and pond skaters, and perhaps even some dragonflies or damselflies if the pond was kick-started with some water from an established pond. Water snails can be obtained from a specialist water-garden nursery and will add to the richness of the wildlife present, grazing on algae and laying their eggs on the underside of floating leaves.

Towards the end of the summer you will have to start preparing the pond for the autumn. Unless your pond is intended to be completely natural then dying and decaying leaves and seed-pods should be removed as they form, to reduce the rate at which a layer of decaying material is built up. Periodically, perhaps every three or four years, the pond will have to be emptied and the detritus removed. The water level in the pond should be maintained by regular topping up, as evaporation from the surface and the leaves of plants will be high in warm weather.

Above: *Newts are an interesting addition to a garden pond, but do consume large amounts of frogspawn.*

Below: *A pond with fully grown marginal plants is a fine garden feature and good for birds.*

Pests and predators

The domestic cat remains the most potent predator in the garden. During late spring and early summer, when the young birds have recently left the nest and still lack the 'street-wisdom' of their parents, cats catch more small birds than at any other time.

There is nothing that can be done to change feline habits – cats are natural predators, and the only action to reduce the slaughter is preventative. For example, bells can be attached to cats' collars, or – if your own cat is the culprit – it can be kept indoors at critical times in the early morning and at dusk. Also take care when siting bird baths, tables, and feeders.

Cats are not the only danger to young garden birds. Avian predators will also be actively searching for prey at this time of year. Sparrowhawks, Kestrels and Tawny Owls all have hungry families to feed. Although it can be upsetting to see a young songbird taken by one of these species, they are the natural predators of small birds, and rely for their own survival on this ready source of food. The same can not be said of Grey Squirrels, and steps should be taken to protect nest boxes from their attentions by screwing a square metal plate with a suitably sized hole over the entrance hole of the nest box. This will also prevent Great Spotted Woodpeckers from enlarging the hole to reach the eggs or nestlings inside.

Clipped hedges and dense evergreens provide good sites for nests. Vulnerable nests can be protected temporarily by nylon mesh placed over the bush or hedge – the adult birds will still be able to access the nest from below. Studies of increased Crow and Magpie populations, which both regularly rob nestlings and eggs, show that predation is rarely to the level where they affect the local population. A dog in the garden will offer some protection to garden birds by scaring off larger predatory birds and cats.

In spite of all these threats, the greatest cause of mortality for young birds once they leave the nest is cold and starvation during their first autumn and winter.

Above: *Young birds are very vulnerable to cats during the first few weeks after leaving the nest.*

Left: *Sparrowhawks often perch on 'plucking posts' when removing feathers from their prey.*

Key summer species

At the start of the summer the breeding season is in full swing, some birds having only just arrived. In just over three months most species will have finished breeding and many will have left the garden. Some to begin the long return migration to their winter quarters, others will temporarily leave the garden to feed on the abundance of food available in the fields and hedgerows.

COMMON KESTREL *Falco tinnunculus*
Length: 31–37cm (12½–15in)

Resident. A small falcon, plumage rusty-brown and buff, blue-grey head in male.

The Kestrel has a very wide distribution in the UK and Ireland, being absent only from the Shetland Isles and scarce in north-west Scotland. It is present in most habitats, although the population in some areas varies considerably, depending on the food supply. The most recent Breeding Atlas (BTO 1993) puts the average British population at about 50,000 pairs. The Kestrel's hunting method is absolutely characteristic. No other small resident bird of prey shares this method of hunting. A high level initial hover is followed by two or more lower level hovers until a final swoop is made down to the ground. The rare Red-footed Falcon and sometimes the Hobby also hover but here it is high up in pursuit of large aerial insects such as dragonflies. The Kestrel is most commonly found in cultivated country with a mixture of fields and pastures and occasional copses and hedges with large trees. In suburbia where there are open spaces it can also be quite common but is also known in the centre of large cities where it nests on tall buildings and tower blocks. Elsewhere advantage is taken of old crow nests and natural cliff ledges. Outside towns the Kestrel's diet consists mainly of rodents but in towns there is a higher proportion of small birds.

Above: *The Kestrel's hunting method makes it easy to identify in flight.*

Below: *Kestrels will use a range of artificial nest sites, located on both trees and man-made structures.*

Above: *The male Kestrel (below) has a blue-grey crown, rump and tail, the back is rich chestnut. The female's (above) is duller brown without the blue-grey on the tail.*

COMMON PHEASANT *Phasianus colchicus*
Length: 55–90cm (22–36in)

Resident. Unmistakable large long-tailed gamebird, male has rich chestnut plumage.

The pheasant is an introduced species, arriving in the UK at about the time of the Normans, having originated in Asia. The annual population is subject to large fluctuations caused by the release of captive-bred birds for shooting. Released birds have a detrimental effect on the population as their breeding success is low and this characteristic is gradually permeating the wild population. The areas of greatest density are where there is a mixture of arable land and patches of woodland and copses, the birds favouring the boundaries between the two zones. In gardens they stay fairly close to the cover of shrubs and denser vegetation. The display of a male Pheasant is a well known sound in early spring in the countryside. A harsh and loud two-syllabic crow is often followed by several wing-beats. Pheasants eat a wide range of vegetable matter, especially preferring the growing shoots of arable crops. Chicks and juveniles also eat a fair number of insects. The nest is placed on the ground in long vegetation on the edge of woodland and the clutch can be very large, normally eight to fifteen but occasionally up to twenty pale green eggs. The young are active as soon as they hatch.

Above: *On the rural fringe of towns and in the country Pheasants are frequent visitors to gardens.*

Right: *The male pheasant* (far right) *is richly coloured, with an exotically marked head. Females are smaller and without the bright colours.*

STOCK DOVE Columba oenas
Length: 31–35cm (12–14in)

Resident. Slim grey pigeon with black on wing and tail tips.

This pigeon has a southerly and easterly distribution in the British Isles. It only reaches as far north as southern Scotland and is absent from most of western and Northern Ireland. It is fairly common in open woodland and cultivated land with a good proportion of trees. Nests are placed in holes in trees but also in nest boxes, where available and buildings. Up to five broods of usually just two white eggs are laid any time between February and November. The song is a repetitive two syllable coo. It feeds exclusively on the ground, chiefly in open fields where it eats a range of berries, seeds and shoots. Its diet is similar to that of the Woodpigeon, and mixed groups are often found feeding together. Like many farmland birds it suffered a decline from the use of organochloride chemicals for seed dressings. Since the ban on these in the early 1960s, the population has partially recovered.

Above: *The Stock Dove's plumage is predominantly grey with a bright green neck patch and pink breast.*

The absence of winter stubble fields in modern agricultural practice has denied the Stock Dove its year-round food supply. There is some evidence that this has caused the long breeding season, replacing a previous June peak in laying. This species can be seen in rural and outer suburban gardens close to parkland.

Above: *In flight, the black trailing edge to the wing with two short black bars is characteristic.*

Left: *Stock Doves suffered a decline due to agricultural chemicals. Following a ban, the population has partially recovered.*

COLLARED DOVE *Streptopelia decaocto*
Length: 31–33cm (12–13in)

Resident. A slim mid-sized dove with pinkish-buff plumage and a black collar.

In the 1930s Collared Doves spread into Europe from Turkey and Yugoslavia and by the early 1950s they were breeding in East Anglia. They are now widespread in the Great Britain, and although less common they are also found throughout Ireland. There are other areas of absence, especially in the mountains and higher moorland. The diet is mainly cereal grains surplus on farms but in gardens birds will take seeds from bird tables and beneath feeders. Like the Stock Dove the Collared Dove in Britain has a long breeding season, from February to early October. Two white eggs are laid in up to five broods a year. The song has become very well known in the suburbs and consists of a three syllable coo with a drawn out and emphasized middle phrase and a rather curtailed final phrase. The population reaches its highest density in the suburbs although there is some indication that breeding success at 26% in the suburbs is somewhat lower than the 41% recorded in rural areas. At first the species was protected, but the close association with humans on farms reduced them to pest status in some locations.

Above: *Collared Doves are common on outer suburban lawns, often taking advantage of the abundant supply of seeds to be found under bird feeders.*

Above: *The white tail tips are noticeable in flight and when the tail is spread.*

Left: *The juvenile Collared Dove* (far left) *does not have the black collar of the adult and has a grayer more scaly-looking plumage.*

COMMON SWIFT *Apus apus*
Length: 16–17cm (6–6½in)

Spring/Summer visitor. All dark, except small white patch on chin and throat. Long scythe-like wings and forked tail.

The sound of Swifts screaming overhead in early August is a reminder that autumn is on its way and that the Swifts will be gone within days. In London their spring arrival and autumn departure en masse seems to be almost on the same date each year. The species is dependent on humans for its nesting sites and small colonies are to be found in tall buildings, wherever the ease of entry and the roof space permit. This is the most aerial of all bird species in Great Britain and Ireland and is entirely dependent on the insects that it is able to catch on the wing. This clearly has an impact on its distribution and it is most common in the warmer and drier south of England. The further west and north the thinner the distribution as the weather becomes wetter and colder and less suitable for flying insects. Swifts lay a single brood of two or three white eggs in mid-May or June depending on the availability of insects. The incubation and fledging periods are variable in length, again depending on the number of flying insects, incubation varies from 19–27 days while fledging follows after a further five to eight weeks. Long flights may be undertaken during breeding if there is bad weather local to the nest. Chicks are able to survive several days without food when the weather is bad, becoming torpid until they are fed again. Once they leave the nest the chicks are no longer fed by the parents and are independent, leaving soon afterwards for the migration to their wintering quarters.

Above: *Screaming parties of Swifts are common over city sky lines on summer evenings.*

Left: *The Swift is the most aerial of British species, feeding, sleeping and even mating on the wing*

PIED WAGTAIL *Motacilla alba*
Length: 17–18cm (6½–7in)

Resident. Small unmistakable black, white and grey bird with round body and long tail.

There are two races of this species. In Great Britain and Ireland and on the near continent the male of the 'Pied' race has an all-black back in the summer whereas in the 'White' race found in the rest of Europe the male's black crown and nape contrasts with a clean mid-grey mantle. The White Wagtail is a common overshooting migrant in the spring in the UK especially in the south and east of the country. The Pied Wagtail is found throughout Great Britain and Ireland and has successfully occupied a very wide range of habitats. It is relatively common in towns and cities and in the country prefers mixed farms. In the recent status report on the UK's birds (RSPB/BTO 2007) there is a 45% increase since 1970. There is some evidence of a decrease in south-eastern Britain. This appears to be due to the switch from mixed to arable farming. The Pied Wagtail is frequently found near water, favouring sewage farms, waterworks and reservoirs where it finds its staple diet of small midge larvae. The call is diagnostic, often made in flight, it sounds as if it is repeatedly calling 'chiswick', 'chiswick'. It forms communal roosts outside the breeding season, often around buildings and sometimes with over 100 birds present. Nesting is carried out between April and August. Usually two broods of from three to five whitish eggs, freckled brown are laid in a cup-shaped nest of roots, moss and grasses. The nest can be placed in a hole or on a ledge located in a wall or building. The incubation and fledging periods are both about fourteen days, typical for a bird of this size.

Above: *The pattern of the juvenile mirrors that of the adult except that it is in grey, brown and white.*

Right: *Male and female Pied Wagtails are similar except the female (below) has a grey back and less black on the head.*

BLACKBIRD *Turdus merula*
Length: 24–27cm (9½–11in)

Resident. Males all black with yellow bill and eye-ring. Female variable brown-grey or rufous.

The Blackbird is among our best known and best loved garden birds. The species is found throughout Great Britain and Ireland, only reducing in density in

the higher mountainous and moorland areas. It is very adaptable and will occupy a wide range of habitat niches. In a garden context it is found everywhere, from inner city areas to the most rural. The population has declined by about 16% since 1970; this reduction has occurred mainly in rural areas and is due to changing agricultural practice.

Below: *Autumn is a time when Blackbirds feed on a wide range of wild berries.*

Singing starts early in the year and the song is delivered from a prominent perch, tree, TV aerial or roof-top. The song is rich and varied, consisting of a series of deliberate clear fluted phrases interspersed with frequent pauses. The nest, which is built from twigs, grass and roots lined with mud and grasses, is placed in hedges, garden shrubs, and ivy, and sometimes in sheds. Two or three broods are raised each consisting of four or five bluish-green eggs speckled with reddish-brown. Incubation and fledging both take about two weeks. A wide range of food is eaten, including insects, worms, snails, fruit, berries and seeds. A similarly wide selection of garden offerings are also taken loose either on the ground or from the bird table. The species is a partial migrant and can be extremely common on the east coast, arriving from northern and eastern Europe in late September.

Above left: *A Blackbird's varied diet includes worms and berries.*

Left: *The Blackbird is one of Britain's most familiar garden song birds.*

STARLING *Sturnus vulgaris*
Length: 20–22cm (8–9in)

Resident and migrant. Adults glossy black plumage, pale spots and shot with lilac and green.

The distinctive appearance and the sociable but quarrelsome manner make the Starling one of the most familiar of our garden birds. Numbers have declined by nearly 73% since 1970 (RSPB/BTO, 2007), this is true across virtually the whole of northern Europe and has been caused by the intensification of and changes to agricultural methods. The most recent UK breeding census (BTO, 1993) shows it to be still present across virtually the whole of Britain and Ireland and missing only on uplands and moorlands as a breeding bird. As the distribution suggests, it is present as a garden bird both in town and country. Although originally a farmland and woodland species, the Starling has successfully adapted to the development of large conurbations. The adults feeds principally by foraging on grassland for insects and worms, also feeding on berries, seeds and fruits in the autumn. The species is notable for the formation of occasionally massive post-breeding flocks when foraging for food. At roost these flocks can number several hundred thousand birds. The late summer and early autumn influx into the UK from northern Europe is on a very large scale and in the past has involved the formation of enormous flocks, with thousands of birds streaming into city centres to

Above: *Large pre-roost flights of Starlings are familiar in autumn over both town and countryside.*

Below: *The dull grey-brown juvenile Starling (right) is very different from the glossy black adult (left).*

roost on the ledges of buildings. Starlings are hole-nesters and will use artificial nest sites. One or two broods of four or five green-blue eggs are laid in April to May, incubation takes about twelve days and a further 21 days elapse before the chicks fledge. Unlike the adults, which are mainly ground-feeders, young birds feed in bushes and trees, possibly because the bill has not yet enough strength for the vigorous probing carried out by the adults. The song is rich and varied with a range of whistles, clicks, squeaks and some high quality mimicry.

HOUSE SPARROW *Passer domesticus*
Length: 14–16cm (6in)

Resident. Closely associated with humans. Small, brown and grey and finch-like.

The House Sparrow is another farmland species that has suffered a significant decline over the past thirty years; the size of the decline, at about 65%, is close to that of the previous species, the Starling. Predation may also have had some impact on the overall population level. Domestic cats and Tawny Owls are both significant predators and in recent years the recovery of Sparrowhawk numbers may also have had an effect. In spite of this, the House Sparrow is nationally common and widespread and is missing only from the higher upland parts of the country. On a more local scale, however, it is no longer seen in some areas or at least seems to be missing for part of the year. The House Sparrow is very closely associated with man and nests mostly in holes in buildings, regularly visiting gardens. Modern building practice has probably reduced significantly the number of suitable nest sites. The highest densities are found where there is a mixture of different buildings having suitable nest sites, which are close to open parkland, or green areas where insects and grubs suitable for feeding youngsters can be found. Adult House Sparrows are primarily seed-eaters but

Above: *Male House Sparrows display by drooping their wings and puffing out their black bib.*

also eat shoots and flowers. They can be pests on farmland, taking seeds from crops in fields. The species is gregarious and noisy with frequent disputes over food or nesting material. Their call consists of a great range of chirruping and chattering sounds that are constantly changing. Several broods can be laid during a season, up to four clutches of three to five white eggs with brown blotches are laid from March to September. Artificial nest sites are used and tits can be displaced from enclosed boxes if the entrance hole is large enough. Nest sites are also used as winter roosts.

Left: *The male House Sparrow* (above) *is handsomely marked in grey, white and brown with a black bib; the female* (below) *is much duller.*

Below: *House Sparrows dust-bathe in summer to rid themselves of parasites.*

BULLFINCH *Pyrrhula pyrrhula*
Length: 14–15cm (5½–6in)

Resident. Chunky finch with deep, stubby, black bill. Male has brilliant rosy red breast and belly.

The Bullfinch is fairly widely distributed but not reported much from gardens owing to its retiring nature, despite the bright colours of the male bird. In the BTO Garden BirdWatch Survey it has been recorded in only 6% of the participating gardens. It is a bird of woodland, scrub, plantations, orchards and the larger gardens of the outer suburbs. It often visits gardens during winter and in spring prior to the first leaves where it feeds on buds, especially flower buds. In more rural areas with commercial orchards, damage to fruit crops can occur. At other times of the year, seeds from plants mainly classified as weeds are taken and the reduction of such seeds owing to changes in farming practice has contributed to a decline of 51% in Bullfinch numbers in the past thirty seven

The male Bullfinch (above) has bright red underparts, while the female (left) is a greyish-buff.

years (RSPB/BTO, 2007). In the autumn fresh fruits and seeds from various trees and shrubs are important in its diet. As in the case of many other seed-eaters, the young are fed on insects. The nest is built in a dense hedge and is constructed from small twigs, roots, moss and hair. At least two broods are laid, from late April onwards, each of four to five green-blue eggs with brownish-purple spots. Incubation and fledging both take about two weeks. Unusually, the Bullfinch maintains its pair bond throughout the year. Paired birds can be seen together in all seasons. The call of this species is diagnostic and is a soft whistle with a downward inflection. The BTO Garden BirdWatch Survey shows that the Bullfinch is almost entirely absent from gardens in the autumn.

Below: *The black, white and grey pattern on the male Bullfinch is distinctive in flight. Females and juveniles share the white rump patch.*

Right: *Juveniles lack the black cap and are dull brown.*

Autumn

Autumn is a season of change with large-scale movements of birds underway in preparation for the harder times to come.

Slowly, as the leaves begin to change colour and fall, and as food resources in the fields, woods and hedges are eaten, we start to notice the birds returning to the garden in late autumn. It is, of course, quite possible that the Greenfinches in our gardens from late autumn and through winter are not the same individuals as those that bred here in the summer. Many of our common bird species migrate south and west to be replaced by continental birds that spend the winter here. For wildlife gardeners wishing to develop their gardens, the autumn is the time when plans conceived during the summer can be carried out. The soil should be easier to dig due to autumn rain. Now you can construct the pond that you have designed or plant the shrubs and trees that you hope will attract more wildlife visitors. Migration continues throughout this period; by late autumn virtually all summer visitors have departed and winter thrushes arrive in force. By the end of the autumn, garden feeding stations and bird tables are much more popular. The really busy season for feeding garden birds is just about to start.

Above: Great Spotted Woodpeckers are often absent from the garden in late summer and early autumn, returning in late autumn. Right: Jays hoard large numbers of acorns in the autumn, for use in the winter.

Feeding Garden Birds

The autumn is the season when many birds are least in need of the food that you provide at your feeding station. There is an abundance of natural food available, so this is the time of year when many of our more common garden bird species are either absent from the garden or present in greatly reduced numbers.

These seasonal variations in garden bird attendance show up very clearly in the BTO's *Garden BirdWatch Book* which published the results to date of the Garden BirdWatch Survey. Many of the finches, Starlings, woodpeckers and pigeons are at their lowest level of reporting in the survey results for the autumn months. Woodland and hedgerows are full of natural food and that is where many of our garden birds are to be found.

If you have been careful in your choice of garden plants and your wildlife gardening plantings provide some of the same seeds and fruits that the birds are feeding on in the wider world outside, then they will continue to visit.

Examples of shrubs and small trees that will provide a supply of natural fruits in late summer and autumn are listed opposite.

Above: *Blackcaps take full advantage of the abundant supply of autumn fruits and seeds.*

NATURAL FRUITS

Berberis	Prolific berries, two evergreen forms
Bramble	Blackberry, available in several forms
Buckthorn	Native shrub, thrives on coast
Cotoneaster	Several species, chose as appropriate
Elder	Common native, small tree, can prune
Hawthorn	Large native shrub, good for thrushes
Holly	Many species, chose as appropriate
Rose sp.	Choose native species, produces hips
Rowan	Medium native tree. Many berries
Pyracantha	Firethorn, ornamental shrub, many berries
Wild Cherry	Small fruits taken by many species
Yew	Native tree, (note: poisonous to humans)

Above right: *Fruits on native trees are a great attraction to birds in the autumn.*

Right: *The commoner tits feed in gardens throughout the year.*

Obviously it will only be possible to have plants from the above list if you have space. If space is at a premium please make sure that you properly research the ultimate size of your potential purchase and chose the plant most appropriate for your situation. In addition to the above and again if space permits a number of seed bearing plants could be put in a 'wild patch', these include, thistles, grasses, knapweed, ragwort, nettles, poppies and teasel. These will also attract many invertebrates and provide nectar for adult butterflies and food for their larvae. Finally there are a number of herbaceous perennials and annuals that provide seeds for birds.

November we can normally expect some overnight frosts. Summer visitors are long gone, a large-scale influx of birds from northern Europe is underway and the winter feeding season can begin in earnest.

In the late autumn some birds, such as Nuthatches and Jays, hide away caches of food for winter. Hazelnuts and acorns left on the bird table could attract both of these species. Jays have been known to collect and store up to 2000 acorns for use later in the winter.

If your garden or its boundaries contain hawthorn bushes then you could have visits from winter thrushes such as Redwing and Fieldfare. These species will be in the country or on the fringes of towns and cities, not moving into the suburbs until later in the winter when the supply of berries begins to run out. Windfall apples left on lawns will often attract both of these thrush species as well as Blackbirds, Song and Mistle Thrushes.

Over-ripe fruit can also be placed on the bird-table where it will readily be eaten by starlings and other species. If there is an area of your lawn that you don't mind getting a bit messy then you can sprinkle seed and it will be eaten by stubble feeding birds such as Chaffinches. In severe weather this could attract unusual species such as Brambling and Tree Sparrow.

Bird tables and loose feeding

In the early autumn it is usually not necessary to provide much food for birds. As already discussed, many birds are absent from the garden, preferring to feed in woodland, hedgerows and on farmlands. By the middle of the autumn the weather will be changing and by the end of

Above: *Starlings and thrushes readily eat over-ripe fruit placed on the ground for them.*

Below: *Bramblings, like other ground feeding birds, take full advantage of fallen fruits and seeds.*

Feeders

By the end of the autumn birds have returned to gardens and are taking seed and nuts from feeders at rates approaching those encountered in the winter. This is especially true if the weather is bad, with early frosts.

The winter is, obviously, the time when the greatest amount of food is taken from garden feeding stations, so if you regularly buy seeds and peanuts you might like to make considerable savings by purchasing in bulk at the beginning of the season, in the autumn. The names and addresses of some specialist garden bird food suppliers are listed in the Useful Addresses section on page 124.

There is some merit in hanging several feeders in a group. Birds often seem to prefer feeding in a flock rather than widely separated and there will be a useful concentration of spilt seed beneath the feeders for the ground-feeders, such as Dunnocks. Sometimes quite large flocks of birds, for example Collared Doves, can be seen foraging beneath hanging feeders. If your garden can accommodate a change, then it is also good practice to move the group of feeders periodically. Remove loose shell husks and fork or rake over the grass or soil underneath, then give it time to recover.

Above right: Bullfinches sometimes visit seed feeders in the late autumn to supplement their natural diet of plant seed-heads.

Right: Young birds, such as this juvenile Nuthatch, visit gardens for the first time in autumn.

Water in the garden

The demand for water is still quite high, especially in early autumn if there is a prolonged spell of fine weather. This is a season with a great many comings and goings – summer visitors leaving, arrivals from northern Europe – and all of the birds involved in these movements will want their plumage to be in tip-top condition for the journey. This means a lot of bathing and preening of feathers.

At peak times my main bird bath has required refilling two or more times a day. An alternative for an exceptionally busy bath is to lay in a permanent section of hose so that it can be filled remotely with a minimum of disturbance. If you do this remember to remove the hose prior to the start of the first frosts otherwise the hose may become iced up and split.

For those of you lucky enough to have a small stream running though your garden now is a good time to make any modifications to help birds gain access to the water. Excavate a small shallow area in a couple of places and line the water's edge with large pebbles. If this layer of pebbles is sufficiently thick you can suppress weed growth on your little beach! Later in the autumn the demand for water will have diminished somewhat, but still remember to change the water frequently and keep your bird-baths clear of autumn leaves.

Above: *House Sparrows will continue to use water for bathing throughout the autumn.*

Below: *Early autumn weather can be warm and create high demand for bathing.*

Ponds

In early autumn the marginal and floating vegetation in the pond should be in good condition, with some plants still flowering. This healthy growth still has a fairly high demand for water, and if the weather is also hot, the pond will have to be topped up from time to time.

As the autumn progresses and plants begin to die back you will need to remove dead leaves from all of the plants in the pond, including the submerged oxygenators. If this is not done, the decaying vegetation forms a silt layer in the pond, hastening the point at which the pond has to be emptied and the sludge cleared out. Oxygenators should be cut back to just a few inches of growth and the cut vegetation removed. When the leaves of the marginal plants have been browned by frost, these too should be cut back and removed to prevent them falling into the pond.

At the same time, examine the containers and cut back and remove superfluous roots and shoots. If the basket has become too full then take out the plant, split it and replant it with fresh soil.

The need to clear out the pond will not arise very often and it is certainly not an annual chore. When it is necessary, the best time for a clear out is in the early part of the growing season.

The final task before the onset of winter for a small or

Above: *Clearing fallen leaves from the pond is a late autumn task and on warmer days Pond Skaters* (below) *will still be active on the water surface.*

medium-sized pond is to spread a net over the top, anchored in place around the edge with heavy stones. This will collect falling leaves and prevent them from decaying in the pond.

The netting should be removed later in the year when the leaves have ceased to be a problem. I once left the net on past the New Year and went into the garden on a January morning to find a perplexed looking frog in the middle of the net. Early to mid December is probably a suitable time.

Migration

In contrast to the sudden arrival of migrants in the spring, the autumn movement south appears to be a long drawn-out affair. Keener birdwatchers will be looking for signs of birds leaving or flying through from early July onwards.

The first birds on the move will not usually be noticed by observers based in gardens; they are mostly wading birds, high Arctic-breeders that can be seen on freshwater marshes and coastal mudflats. By mid-August, however, things have started to happen on a wider front. Town and city dwellers will notice the absence of their local colony of swifts – in London the bulk of these have departed by the second week of August. By the middle of September, local breeding warblers such as Chiffchaffs or Blackcaps are no longer to be seen in most of the UK. Swallows and martins leave over a far more protracted period, from August through to October or even later in southern coastal areas.

People who live by the sea in the south and particularly the east of the country will be familiar with the large influxes of birds that arrive from time to time on the coast. Birds migrating south along the continental coast and over the North Sea get caught up in weather fronts crossing their path and are diverted in large numbers onto the east coast of Britain. The numbers of birds involved in these 'falls' can be truly colossal, sometimes hundreds of thousands or even millions.

Above: *The Blackcap is one of several species that can arrive in very large numbers.*

Left: *More unusual visitors can be seen, like this Black Redstart on the East Coast.*

Above: *House Martins gather into large flocks, resting on buildings and feeding on the last insects of the autumn prior to their long migration overland to southern Africa.*

Different species have evolved very different strategies for migration. Many small birds move south in relatively small flights feeding as they go. When they reach a large natural barrier such as a mountain range or a sea crossing they will feed heavily and increase their body weight with a lot of fat. This fat is then burnt up in the longer flight that will be required. Others, more aerial by nature, such as swifts undertake much longer flights. There are also many theories concerning navigation on these long flights.

Seabirds also undertake very long migrations, the world record holder for the species having the longest migration is held by the Arctic Tern, which breeds in Northern England and Scotland. This species spends the winter in the Antarctic Ocean and a bird ringed in the UK has been recorded in Australia. If you live near the coast, you may be lucky enough to see some of these massive movements of many different types of seabird and be the first to welcome winter visitors such as Redwings and Fieldfares to your garden.

In this section we look at mainly long distance migrants that make journeys to Africa and out into the South Atlantic. In the next section we shall concentrate on more local movements.

Right: *Many Chiffchaffs from continental Europe arrive in autumn, some staying to spend the winter.*

Regional movements

Migration is a very complex affair and in the autumn it takes place over a number of months. Not all of the birds arriving and leaving are long-distance migrants; many of our common garden birds undertake shorter migrations, moving south and west for the winter. Others, like the various gull species that we are familiar with, breed on the coast and move inland to spend the winter scavenging around town and city rubbish tips and dumps.

Britain has a maritime climate and enjoys warmer winter weather than northern Europe. Many millions of birds take advantage of the difference in temperature and cross the North Sea to spend the winter in the British Isles. Large numbers of thrushes join our resident birds, crossing from the near continent and Iceland by the million. Some of the birds will be species like Blackbird and Song Thrush and impossible to separate from our breeding birds of the same species. Others, such as Redwing and Fieldfare, are very different and can be quite easily separated from our breeding species. They are both rare breeding birds in the UK and the majority of the Redwings and Fieldfares arriving in late September and October come from northern Europe, with some Redwings also from Iceland. Initially, these thrushes will

Above: *Black-headed Gulls migrate from the coast in autumn, gathering on inland lakes and waterways.*

be found in the country feeding on the crop of hawthorn and other berries, but they begin to move into towns and outer suburbs as berry stocks are exhausted.

Thrushes are not the only species arriving during the autumn. Skylarks, finches, pipits and Goldcrests all descend in large numbers on the east coast. Later in the year, some species like the Siskin become regular visitors to our bird feeders. Very small numbers of Chiffchaffs and Blackcaps also arrive from the continent to spend the winter in sheltered areas and can be seen from time to time in suburban gardens. Most Chiffchaffs and Blackcaps fly south and spend the winter in southern Europe and north Africa.

Offsetting the large numbers of arriving birds, a percentage of our common garden birds move west and south into France and southern Europe for the winter. These large-scale changes bring the inevitable territorial disputes and some species, like Robins, can be observed fighting over winter feeding territories during the autumn.

Less noticeable to garden-based observers are the small numbers of larger birds that also arrive – Long-eared and Short-eared Owls, various birds of prey and Bitterns come in quantities that vary from year to year. On the coasts, thousands of wading birds come and spend the winter on our mudflats and estuaries. If you have a coastal garden, you will be familiar with the daily flights of these birds as they move to and from their feeding grounds in response to the movements of the tides.

Below: *Starlings gather into large flocks, migrating locally to take advantage of any feeding opportunity.*

Pests and predators

As the autumn moves into winter, cats become less of a threat to garden birds. Leaves have fallen from trees and shrubs, making cats more visible, young birds are beginning to acquire some survival skills and the cats themselves are spending more time indoors as the weather cools down.

The feeding tempo at the bird table and on the garden feeders is picking up and occasional garden birds will be taken by avian predators, such as Sparrowhawks or, especially in city areas, Kestrels. In contrast to cats, these are natural predators and the small numbers of birds that are taken do not usually affect overall populations.

Careful siting of the bird table and feeders will reduce the number of birds taken, if predators become a problem. The table should be positioned close to cover but not so that a cat can approach undetected and it should be at least 1.5 m above the ground. Feeders can be hung in a group and the birds will then feed in a flock – this will make it easier for them to spot an approaching Sparrowhawk and take evasive action. The birds taken by an avian predator tend to be the weaker members of the flock, a process that ensures survival of the fittest.

Above: *The Sparrowhawk is a natural predator, taking small numbers of small birds from gardens.*

Below: *Siting your bird table in the open away from cover reduces the threat from predatory cats.*

Key autumn species

Migration of one species or another will be in progress throughout the autumn months. At the start of the period it will mean the departure of summer visitors like Willow Warbler and Spotted Flycatcher. By the end of the autumn there will have been large movements of larks, pipits and finches and the winter thrushes will have arrived *en masse*.

WOODPIGEON *Columbia palumbus*
Length: 38–45cm (15–18in)

Above: *Roosts of Wood Pigeons can be very large.*

Resident. Large grey pigeon with prominent white wing-bar and neck marking, breast pinkish.

The Woodpigeon is a common garden bird throughout the British Isles, it is missing only in the more mountainous parts of the country. As might be expected, the highest concentrations are found in arable farmland, but it can also be found in parkland in city centres. In contrast with the decline in many farmland birds, the most recent RSPB/BTO study found that the Woodpigeon's numbers have increased since the 1970s by 110%. It is now found in parks and gardens and is no longer the shy retiring bird of open country and woodland edges that it was in the past. A wide range of food is eaten: peas, beans and brassicas such as cabbages and sprouts, and in the autumn haws, acorns, beech mast and elderberry are all taken. It is easy to see why farmers regard the Woodpigeon as a pest. In the garden it will eat most loose offerings, usually on the ground but also at the bird table. Its large size makes it a bit of a bully and it tends to dominate smaller birds. The Woodpigeon has an extended breeding season and has been recorded nesting in all months of the year; the usual period, however, is from May to September. It normally has two broods, laying two eggs per brood and takes seventeen days to incubate them. Fledging can take from three to five weeks, depending on the availability of food. Its cooing breeding song is distinctive as is the clapping noise it makes with its wings when disturbed from a tree. Woodpigeons are partial migrants, with large numbers of northern European birds spending the winter in the UK.

Left: *The Wood Pigeon is the largest British pigeon and can take a lot of feeding.*

FERAL PIGEON *Columbia livia*
Length: 31–35cm (12–14in)

Resident. A medium-sized dove with a very wide range of colours; some are like Rock Doves.

The ancestor of the Feral Pigeon is the wild Rock Dove, now found only on the extreme west and north-west of the British Isles. In the past, domesticated Rock Doves have been kept in dovecotes for the table, for message-carrying and more recently for racing. Inbreeding has led to a wide range of colour variations and patterns. Like the Rock Dove, the Feral Pigeon has a nesting preference for ledges and holes. Rock Doves find their nest sites on seacliffs and crags, whereas tall buildings provide a convenient equivalent for their town and city cousins. Nesting takes place from March to September, with two or three broods each of two eggs. Incubation takes about seventeen days and fledging four to five weeks. There is some evidence that pure-bred Rock Doves are reducing in number due to interbreeding with Feral Pigeons and racing birds. In cities, Feral Pigeons are scavengers and the spread of fast-food outlets has probably had some effect on their increase in numbers. In the garden, kitchen scraps, grain and bread are all eaten. The sheer numbers of birds in some city areas causes problems

Above: *A wide range of colours and markings can be seen in Feral Pigeons.*

with the fouling of buildings and the possibility of disease. Large amounts of money are spent by city authorities on culling Feral Pigeons and introducing measures to deter them from using certain buildings.

Above: *Flocks of feral pigeons are widespread in towns and cities.*

Left: *Feral Pigeons are descended from wild Rock Doves and some retain a similar plumage.*

BARN OWL *Tyto alba*
Length: 33–36cm (12½–14in)

Resident. Medium size, white underparts and underwing obvious in flight, upperparts spangled yellow-brown.

The Barn Owl has been in long-term decline in Great Britain and Ireland. It is difficult to census and is subject to annual fluctuations in numbers owing to the cyclical population of voles, its main prey. As farming methods have become more intensive and suitable hunting habitat has become more scarce, numbers of Barn Owls have dropped. The organochloride chemicals that had such an impact in the 1950s on birds of prey also affected Barn Owls. The species is very much a bird of open agricultural and rough grazing land with scattered copses and woods. Only those gardens situated in such areas will be familiar with its elegant, ghostly evening hunting flight over open meadows and along hedges and ditches. At most times of the year it can be seen only late in the evening; otherwise it is nocturnal. Its main prey items are voles but frogs, insects and some small birds are also taken. The Barn Owl nests in holes in trees or buildings and is

Above: *Prey items are often eaten on the ground. This bird is 'mantling' with its wings to protect its food.*

a regular user of nest boxes when provided in farm buildings. One or two broods of from four to seven white eggs are laid between March and July. Incubation and fledging periods are lengthy, taking 33 days and ten weeks respectively. Its distribution in Great Britain and Ireland is patchy and shows a significant reduction when the 1968–72 and 1988–91 Atlas results are compared.

Barn Owls use regular perches to search for prey (left) and have feathers specially adapted for silent flight (below).

TAWNY OWL *Strix aluco*
Length: 36–40cm (14–16in)

Resident. Medium sized, compact owl with broad, rounded wings. Colour is a mottled rufous-brown.

The Tawny Owl is the most familiar of the British owls and is found throughout England, Scotland and Wales but is totally absent from Ireland. It is mainly a woodland species but is also common on agricultural land and in suburban gardens where there are mature trees and secure nesting and roosting sites. It is nocturnal and will be mostly known for its call and 'song'. The commonest call is a shrill 'kewick' used to maintain contact, the song is a very familiar mournful hooting noise. Tawny Owls are at their most vocal in late autumn or early winter when they are establishing their territory. The nesting period is from February to

Above: *Glimpsed at dusk, the rounded wings and large head of a Tawny Owl make a distinctive flight silhouette.*

June and a single brood of two to four white eggs is laid and takes about thirty days to incubate. The fledging period is a further four or five weeks, the young birds will not be fully independent until about three months after leaving the nest. In areas where natural nest sites are in short supply, Tawny Owls will use artificial nests usually in the form of a long chimney-like box slung underneath a large branch about 5–10 m above the ground. In rural areas the diet is almost exclusively small rodents but, like Kestrels, in town they take a high proportion of small birds. Tawny Owls often have an established favourite roost tree where they pass the daylight hours close to the trunk hidden by foliage or ivy. The presence of a roosting owl is sometimes given away by 'mobbing' noises from small birds, which have discovered the dozing bird.

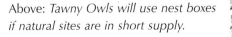

Above: *Tawny Owls will use nest boxes if natural sites are in short supply.*

Right: *Young Tawny Owls take three months to reach independence after leaving the nest.*

GREY WAGTAIL *Motacilla cinerea*
Length: 18–20cm (7–8in)

Resident. Small grey-backed bird with long tail constantly pumped, bright yellow under tail.

The Grey Wagtail is widespread throughout Britain and Ireland although it is very scarce in lowland midland and eastern parts of England. This is due to its preference for fast-flowing streams close to deciduous trees. If you are lucky enough to live where there is such a stream, you will be familiar with the fly-catching activities of the Grey Wagtail. A wide range of insects is taken as food and it is this that determines its preference for streams bordered by broad-leaved trees rather than conifers or moorland. There is a higher variety and greater number of insects available at such sites. Nests are built in rocky crevices in either natural locations between boulders or in man-made equivalents such as stone bridges, mills or lock buildings. Two broods are usually laid and raised between April and late July, each clutch being of four or five off-white eggs finely speckled with grey. Incubation and fledging each take about two weeks. The Grey Wagtail is mostly sedentary with a small number of migrants from northern Europe entering the country. There is some evidence of an altitudinal movement of birds down from the hills and mountains, especially in northern England and Scotland.

Above: *Grey Wagtails are invariably associated with water, especially rivers and streams.*

Below: *Grey Wagtails often build their nests under stone bridges over water.*

Above: *Running water is preferred and this influences the Grey Wagtails distribution.*

ROBIN *Erithacus rubecula*
Length: 13-15cm (5–6in)

Resident. Small plump bird with bright red breast, dark grey-brown mantle and wings and white belly.

The Robin is probably Britain's best known and best loved garden bird. It has won this position by a combination of its attractive appearance and its confiding nature. The BTO Atlas of Breeding Birds (BTO 1993) shows that only in Shetland and Orkney is it scarce and in the rest of the British Isles it was present in virtually every recording square. A suburban garden, with its mixture of lawns and borders of shrubs, is a very suitable habitat for Robins. In the wild they are almost entirely insectivorous, feeding on a variety of small invertebrates, but they will take a range of items at a garden feeding station. Bird-cake consisting of crushed peanuts, milled oats and bound together with fat makes an ideal high energy food for Robins. They like grated cheese, while a bowl of mealworms will quickly make you a friend for life!

A Robin's song is a fluent mixture of thin squeaky notes with varied speed and pitch and very little repetition. The call is a hard, brief 'tic', which extends into a long, protracted sequence when the bird is alarmed. Nests are open and placed close to the ground in a bramble or equivalent. Two broods are raised between April and July, consisting of five or six whitish eggs speckled finely with red. Incubation and fledging both take about two weeks. The juvenile birds are the source of much confusion, initially having a finely spotted buffy-brown breast and looking little like their parents.

Above: *The Robin is one of the few birds that sings all year round.*

Resident British Robins are joined each autumn by an influx of birds from northern Europe. Robins are territorial for most of the year and this influx in the autumn is the cause of many disputes. The species is extremely aggressive in defence of its territory and occasionally a persistent rival will cause a fight with a fatal outcome.

Below: *Young Robins* (right) *are very different in appearance to adults* (left) *and can cause confusion to inexperienced birdwatchers.*

GOLDCREST *Regulus regulus*
Length: 8–9cm (3½in)

Resident. Very tiny, restless bird, olive-green above, buff beneath, yellow crown stripe, bordered black.

The Goldcrest is common throughout Great Britain and Ireland, absent only in areas without any trees. In the breeding season in conifers it can be extremely numerous and comprise more than 30% of the total number of birds present. In spite of its tiny size, it is able to survive in very harsh conditions. It is a partial migrant, and large numbers of Goldcrests reach the east coast in the autumn. It feeds on the smallest of insects, which it is able to pick off tree bark with its needle-like bill. If you have conifers in or near your garden, Goldcrests are likely to be visitors, usually mixed up in a flock of tits with which they often associate in autumn and winter. Goldcrests often give away their presence by their high-pitched 'zee-zee' call notes that they use to keep in contact with the other birds. They do visit bird tables, especially in bad weather, where they

take fat, cheese and crumbs. The nest is invariably in conifers and is made from moss and lichens bound together with spiders' webs and suspended beneath a branch. Two clutches of eight to ten whitish eggs with brown spots are laid from April onwards. The incubation period is about fifteen days and the fledging period up to twenty days. This high rate of production is necessary because winter mortality is high. Sometimes, on cold winter nights, when they can lose up to 20% of their body weight in staying warm, they have been known to roost in a huddle to conserve heat.

Above: *Goldcrests usually build their nest suspended from the branches of a conifer.*

Left: *In autumn and winter Goldcrests often roam the woods in mixed flocks of tits.*

MARSH TIT *Parus palustris*
Length: 11-12cm (4½-5in)

Resident. Blue Tit size, grey above, off-white beneath with black cap and bib, cheeks white.

Above: *Marsh Tits are occasional visitors to larger and more rural gardens.*

The Marsh Tit is very similar to the Willow Tit and extremely difficult to separate, song and calls being the easiest way. Neither is a regular garden visitor and the recent BTO and RSPB study into the status of Britain's Birds (RSPB/BTO 2007) shows that the population of each has declined by an alarming 60–70% in the past thirty years. This species is likely only to be known in rural areas where it frequents open deciduous wood-land, parks and larger gardens, often near the presence of water. Its distribution in the British Isles is limited to England and Wales and even here it is missing in several areas. It is extremely sedentary and there are no incoming winter migrants from northern Europe to swell the population. Marsh Tits feed on insects and various seeds, including those of herbaceous plants and grasses. It is a cavity nester using holes in trees, Willow Tit nests and sometimes nest boxes. It is usually single-brooded, laying seven or eight white eggs spotted with red-brown at the end of April or in May. Incubation is complete in about two weeks and fledging takes a little longer. In gardens it visits both feeders and tables, taking similar food to the Blue Tit.

Above: *Marsh Tit numbers have declined by over 60% in the past 30 years.*

Left: *Willow Tit differs from Marsh Tit in having a pale panel on its wing. The song and calls are also different.*

Right: *Like all tits they are hole nesters, usually in trees but also in nest boxes.*

COAL TIT *Parus ater*
Length: 10.5–11.5cm (4½in)

Resident. Blue Tit size, olive-grey back, buff beneath, black cap and bib, white cheeks and nape patch.

Coal Tits are birds of coniferous woodland, so if you have conifers in your garden or there are some close by, you could be visited by Coal Tits. The Coal Tit is found throughout Great Britain and Ireland and is missing only from Orkney and Shetland. It is more of a strictly woodland species than Great Tit or and Blue Tit it, preferring conifers – although it can be found in deciduous woods if there are a few conifers present. It has a very distinctive song and can be heard calling a repetitive 'pitchoo, pitchoo, pitchoo' from high in the trees. It feeds on seeds, insects and small spiders, although young Coal Tits are fed exclusively on insects. Northern European populations are dependent on spruce-cone seeds and when the crop of these fails they are prone to irruptive movements in autumn. The Coal Tit appears to be better able to survive in colder conditions than other tits perhaps because of its ability to forage on the underside of snow covered conifer branches and its habit of storing surplus food. The species is a hole-nester, the site chosen usually being placed quite low in the tree. Coal Tits will use nest boxes, having similar nesting requirements to Blue Tits. One or two clutches of seven to eleven white eggs with reddish spots are laid in late April and incubated for seventeen or eighteen days. Fledging takes place after a further sixteen days and the young are independent two weeks later.

Above: *Black sunflower seeds are taken whole from the feeder and opened on a nearby perch.*

Left: *The Coal Tit's white nape is a useful distinguishing feature.*

TREECREEPER *Certhia familiaris*
Length: 12–13cm (4½in)

Resident. Small brown bird with streaky back, off-white beneath and thin, decurved bill.

Treecreepers are woodland birds dependent on large trees with rough insect-rich bark and will only be seen in mature gardens having large trees and adjacent woodland. They creep mouse-like up tree trunks, searching for insects, supported by the stiff spines of their tail feathers. When an upward spiralling search has been completed on one tree they will fly down towards the base of the trunk of the next tree and start again. Their high-pitched call and song matches their mousy appearance. In the winter they will often be seen roaming the wood in a mixed flock of foraging tits. They feed on small insects and spiders taken from crevices in the bark by their perfectly adapted thin, down-curved bill. If Treecreepers are in the neighbourhood of your garden, they can be attracted by smearing a mixture of fat, crushed peanut and seed into the bark cracks of an old fruit tree. They breed during April, May and June, building a nest of small twigs, grasses and moss placed behind a flap of bark or in the crevice of some stonework. One or two clutches of white eggs, spotted brown are incubated for two weeks. Fledging will take a similar amount of time. Treecreepers are sedentary and prone to crashes in population in very severe winters.

Above right:
Treecreepers use their stiff tail feathers to support them when climbing tree trunks.

Right: *Nests are usually placed behind a flap of thick bark.*

JAY *Garrulus glandarius*
Length: 33–36cm (13–14in)

Resident. Small crow, blue patch in grey wing, pinkish breast and belly, white rump.

The Jay is a bird of woodland and is shy and unobtrusive especially during the breeding season. It is relatively widespread throughout England, Wales and southern Scotland but very sparsely spread through northern Scotland and the Northern Isles. They are seen as visitors to gardens mainly in rural areas and the outer suburbs but retain their shy habits and do not usually go far from the cover of trees or bushes. They are closely associated with deciduous woodland and in particular oak trees. The staple diet in the autumn and winter is acorns, which are hoarded in large numbers during September, October and November. This is the time of the year when Jays are most visible. At other times of the year they feed on insects and fruits, and during the breeding season they also take a number of eggs and nestlings of smaller garden birds. They are probably just as effective at nest robbing as the much-reviled Magpie. The alarm call of a Jay is probably heard more often than the bird is seen, consisting of a harsh scream, which warns all other birds of the presence of a predator or human intruder. The nest is an untidy looking affair made of twigs taken from trees, and held together with roots, grasses and hair. Breeding takes place in May and June and from three to seven greenish brown-marked eggs are laid, taking about sixteen or seventeen days to incubate and about three weeks to fledge. Jays are mainly sedentary but do undertake large-scale irruptive movements when there is a failure of the acorn crop.

Above left: *Jays are one of the most colourful birds to visit the garden; their upperwing plumage* (above) *being particularly striking.*

Below: *Jays have been recorded storing up to 2000 acorns* (left), *often foraging in groups on the ground.*

CARRION CROW *Corvus corone*
Length: 45–49cm (18–19in)

Resident. Large all-black crow, aggressive and noisy

The Carrion Crow is found throughout England, Scotland and Wales, being replaced by a two-toned sister species the Hooded Crow in Ireland and north-west Scotland. Where the two species occur at the same place they sometimes interbreed. Crows eat a very wide range of foods and it is this factor that has probably led to their widespread distribution. Although they eat mainly grain in the winter and insects in the summer, they also take a lot of carrion and in the breeding season eggs and young chicks from songbirds. Surplus food is sometimes hoarded, especially in the winter. Everywhere they are regular scavengers at rubbish tips. In rural areas they are shy birds, becoming tamer where they are used to being fed in gardens on bread and kitchen scraps. The nest is a large construction placed high in a tree, usually in a fork; the outer portion is built of twigs, the inner nest

Above: *Carrion Crows are familiar birds in gardens throughout most of Britain.*

lined with roots, earth, hair and grasses. The nesting season lasts from March through to June and a single clutch of four or five greenish eggs with brown markings take about eighteen days to incubate. The lengthy fledging period lasts 32–36 days and there is a further month before the chicks achieve independence.

Left: *Crows have a wide range of body postures used in threat and display.*

Below: *Carrion Crows* (right) *and Rooks* (left) *are a similar size and not easily separated in flight.*

Left: *As their name suggests, Crows eat a lot of carrion such as road kills.*

TREE SPARROW *Passer montanus*
Length: 13.5–14.5cm (5½–6in)

Resident. An attractive grey and brown sparrow with red-brown cap, black cheek spot, white nape band.

Numbers of Tree Sparrows have declined by more than 90% in the past thirty seven years (RSPB/BTO 2007). This is due to changes in farming methods and also to loss of nesting sites owing to the destruction of hedgerows and Dutch elm disease. The Tree Sparrow is a bird of open woodland and cultivated land with clumps of trees and hedgerows. In gardens it will be mainly known in rural areas and small towns and villages, rarely in cities. Its main food is grain and seeds but also insects and spiders. In gardens it will visit bird tables for seeds and kitchen scraps but it is far less noisy and confiding than the House Sparrow. Calls are similar to House Sparrow except for a distinctive nasal 'sewitt' and a 'teck, teck, teck' flight call. Its affinity for trees is due to its hole-nesting habit, although holes in haystacks and buildings are also used. The nest is messily constructed from straw and grasses like that of the House Sparrow. Nest boxes are used but Tree Sparrows are highly susceptible to disturbance. There are usually two broods of four to six eggs laid in late April. Incubation and fledging both take about two weeks.

Above: *The distinctive call is the easiest way to identify Tree Sparrow in flight.*

Below: *Autumn crops of hedgerow fruits are a favourite food for Tree Sparrows.*

CHAFFINCH *Fringilla coelebs*
Length: 14.5–16cm (5½–6½in)

Resident. Male has distinctive pink breast and blue cap, female is a soft grey-brown. Both have white shoulder patch and a wing-bar.

The Chaffinch is common throughout Britain and Ireland and is really scarce only in the Northern Isles. It is one of the commonest British birds and is found wherever there are trees and bushes in both rural and urban situations. It favours broad-leaved woodland but is also found in conifers and has benefited from the increased afforestation of upland areas in the last thirty to forty years. In addition to its tolerance of a wide range of habitat, the Chaffinch also eats a very large variety of food. It feeds mainly on seed taken from the ground – more than 100 types of seed have been recorded in its diet (BTO 1993). With this tolerance of both habitat and

Above: *White wing markings and green rump are distinct in flight.*

food, the Chaffinch is clearly going to take advantage of food available in gardens. It is a regular visitor to feeding stations, where it is more likely to be seen on the ground underneath the bird table and feeders, picking up seeds, bread and cake crumbs dropped by the birds feeding above. Its nesting season is from May until August and in this time it will lay one or two clutches of eggs, blue in colour with purplish markings. Incubation and fledging each take about two weeks. The nest is a very neatly constructed cup made from grass and moss, lined with feathers and decorated on the outside with lichens and spiders' webs. The resident British and Irish population is swollen by a large influx of birds from northern Europe in the autumn.

Above: *Male (above) and female (below) are similarly patterned but the male is much brighter.*

Right: *British and Irish birds are joined by a large influx of continental birds in autumn.*

BRAMBLING *Fringilla montifringilla*
Length: 14–15cm (5½–6in)

Autumn/Winter visitor. Chaffinch size, male has black head and orange breast in summer, female duller.

Bramblings are scarce visitors to gardens in winter months only. They breed in the northern Scandinavian forests and move south in search of their staple winter food, beech-mast. In fact, it is the supply of beech-mast that determines whether or not Bramblings will visit gardens in any particular winter. During the spring and summer they primarily feed on insects and seeds. The BTO Garden BirdWatch handbook showed the seasonality of their visits to gardens and that in most years only 3–5% of the gardens participating in the scheme are visited by Bramblings. Gardens in rural areas or on the outskirts of villages and small towns are most likely to be visited. The common theme though will always be the proximity of beech trees. Bramblings are invariably ground-feeders, flying up into nearby cover when disturbed. Winter flocks can be extremely large and on the continent flocks numbering millions have been recorded (BTO 1986). In this country, however, the flocks are much smaller, usually in the tens and very occasionally hundreds. Their normal arrival time is in October and November and it is worth scanning finch flocks for Bramblings; their white oval rump patch makes them easy to pick out when they are mixed with Chaffinches. Migrating birds are often flying too high for visual identification and are often mixed with Chaffinch. Here the characteristic wheezy 'eeeph' Brambling flight call is useful, which is easily separated from the softer 'yupp' flight call made by Chaffinch.

Above: *In flight, white rump is distinctive.*

Above left: *In winter plumage the male has a grey-brown head, which becomes progressively darker as spring approaches.*

Left: *The Brambling is a winter visitor to the UK from northern Europe.*

GOLDFINCH *Carduelis carduelis*
Length: 11.5–12.5cm (4½–5in)

Resident. Male and females similar, red, black and white head, brown back and yellow wing-bar.

In the past, the striking appearance of the Goldfinch and its sweet song made it a favourite cagebird to the extent that the wild population was reducing. Following a ban on the capture and sale of wild-caught birds the wild population has recovered (BTO 2007). It is found throughout Britain and Ireland except in the north-west of Scotland and the Northern Isles. Although the Goldfinch is to be seen all year round, approximately 80% of the UK population moves onto the continent in September and October to spend the winter in France, Belgium and Spain, returning in April and May. It is a seed-eater throughout the year, taking advantage of different plants each season. In the autumn and winter it is often found in small flocks feeding on teasels and thistles on scrubby weed-covered land. The Goldfinch is seen in gardens throughout the year with a particular peak in April. They readily take to eating black sunflower and Nyjer seeds from a feeder. When they are feeding in a flock they maintain contact by liquid twittering calls, often heard before you can catch a glimpse of the birds themselves. Nesting is from April to August, and a neat cup-shaped nest of roots, moss and lichens is often placed near the end of a branch. Two or three broods can be raised, each clutch consisting of four to six white eggs with red freckles. Incubation takes about twelve to thirteen days and the young birds fledge after a further two weeks.

Thistle (above) and teasel (below) seed heads are favourite foods in the autumn.

Left: *Prior to the moult juveniles are much duller than adults, lacking the distinctive head markings.*

Above: *The broad yellow wing bar makes flight identification simple.*

LINNET *Acanthis cannabina*
Length: 13–14m (5–5½in)

Resident. A compact small finch, male with red forehead and upper breast in spring, russet on back.

The Linnet is common on coastal heaths and occasionally in areas with thick scrub and bushes. It is widespread in the UK and Ireland and absent from western and northern Scotland and the Northern Isles. Linnets are partial migrants, with a proportion of the UK population moving south to Spain to spend the winter. The population of Linnets in the country has reduced by some 57% in the past thirty seven years (BTO, RSPB 2007); this appears to be primarily due to the increased use of herbicides and the consequent reduction in weeds and the small seeds of plants such as buttercup and sorrel that Linnets feed on. In most parts of the country, Linnets will be uncommon or rare garden visitors, probably more often seen in gardens which adjoin areas of heath or open scrubland particularly near the south and east coasts. Encourage them to gardens by not being too worried if dandelion clocks appear in your lawn and flower borders and make sure the food you put out contains a good supply of rape seed, for in the absence of weed seeds Linnets often depend on stubbles of arable crops, especially of oil-seed rape. Winter flocks are active, constantly on the move, keeping contact with a continuous twittering. The nest is placed very low in dense trees or bushes or on the ground and is made of small twigs, stalks and moss and lined with hair, wool and plant down. The first clutch of four to six eggs is laid mainly in April with a preference for evergreens for the first brood. Later broods also use deciduous bushes when the leaves and cover have thickened up. The eggs are pale to whitish-blue speckled and blotched at the broad end with purplish-brown. Incubation and fledging both take about two weeks.

Above: *Linnets in flight – note the typical finch shape and forked tail.*

Left: *Male Linnets are brightly marked in the breeding season with a striking red upper breast and crown.*

REED BUNTING *Emberiza schoeniclus*
Length: 14–15cm (5½–6in)

Resident. Typical bunting with streaked rufous-brown upperparts, white breast and collar; male has black head in spring and summer with white moustache.

Reed Buntings are fairly rare visitors to gardens; only 2% of the participating gardens in the BTO Garden BirdWatch Survey reported their presence in most years. In gardens they were highly seasonal, with a marked peak in late winter/early spring and were almost entirely absent in the breeding season. This is not surprising, as they prefer to nest on or close to the ground in tall dense vegetation with moist soil, typically reedbeds and fens. In recent years they appear to be more frequent visitors to gardens, perhaps owing to the increasing provision of soft sunflower seeds, which are closer to their natural foods. The nesting period is from April/May onwards and the nest is made principally from grasses and lined with finer grasses and hair. Two or three broods are raised in a season and the clutch of four to six bluish eggs takes about two weeks to incubate and another twelve to thirteen days to fledge.

Above: *Females are duller than males, even in winter when the male loses its bold black and white head pattern.*

The call note of the Reed Bunting is a thin drawn out and descending 'Tseeeeu' which once heard is quite distinctive. The song is equally distinct even though it is somewhat variable. It consists of a slow deliberate series of 'chips' with a final faster flourish and is usually delivered from the top of a reed stem or small bush.

The most recent RSPB/ BTO study of the status of Britain's birds reports a 33% drop in Reed Buntings since 1970. This is possibly due to the increased use of herbicides and the consequent drop in the availability of seeds in the winter.

Right: *In winter Reed Buntings can be found feeding far from water on fields and grassy areas.*

Winter

Winter is the season when garden feeding stations really pay dividends in the range and number of visiting birds. The tougher the weather the busier they will be, and the more unusual the birds.

Winter usually arrives in earnest during December, although prolonged cold spells can come much earlier in the north of the country. Birds visit feeders more and more frequently and it is vital to keep up the supply of food for them during really hard weather once they have come to rely on your garden provisions. If you present a variety of foods, some in feeders and some on the ground, then the range of visiting species will increase. In cold snaps garden birdwatchers can sometimes see really large movements of birds taking place. If a period of frost is prolonged and covers much of the country, huge numbers of thrushes, larks and finches can be spurred on to head usually south and west to find better weather and food. If the UK is frost-free and the cold conditions are on the continent, the numbers of birds here will increase greatly. However, these grim times don't last for ever and late winter brings signs of things to come. In February the earliest of the spring bulbs will be in bloom over a large part of the country. Further north, changes happen later, but the arrival of the first spring migrants is only weeks away.

Above: Robins maintain a territory in winter for feeding, which only occasionally break down during very cold snaps. Right: Up to five species of thrush may visit gardens, especially in hard winters.

Attracting birds to your garden

Regular feeding, once established, needs to be maintained during the colder weather. This will ensure the survival of birds that have built their routine around the supply of food you provide. At other times of the year birds can accommodate an interruption in the food supply but in the hardest part of the winter this is much more difficult. Continue to put out food until well into spring when natural food sources will become available once again.

Above: *The winter months are a lean time for birds, and native trees provide a valuable food resource.*

Right: *Pheasants can be seen scratching for food under shrubs and on the lawn.*

If you have chosen your garden plants carefully, some of the shrubs that you have planted in your garden will now have an important part to play and will provide berries and fruits through into the winter. Examples of these are berberis, cotoneaster, hawthorn, ivy and pyracantha. Several native trees are valuable food resources; for example, birch and alder are particularly significant for finches like Siskin and Redpoll, as well as members of the tit family. The plants in the herbaceous border can be left uncut until the end of the winter and will provide a useful supply of seeds for birds such as Goldfinch. Apple trees, especially old ones, are one of the most useful trees in the garden. At the expense perhaps of a smaller crop, avoid spraying them to make the trees

more attractive to a greater number of birds. They support a wide community of insects, which will be a valuable source of food to mixed flocks of tits and other birds. In the spring the blossom is both ornamental and the buds also provide food for Bullfinches. In the autumn and winter the windfall apples are eaten by the thrushes and Starlings. Shelter is especially important in the winter. When all of the deciduous trees have lost their leaves, a few evergreens will provide valuable roosts. In this instance even trees like Leylandii, normally discouraged in small gardens, can be very useful if kept judiciously pruned to encourage bushy growth. Holly is a good shrub for cover and can be especially useful if sited next to the feeding station. The prickly leaves deter predators and offer shelter for roosting birds. Hollies are fairly robust plants and pruning will allow you to develop a shrub with a bare trunk for the first few feet and very thick foliage above this level. In my previous garden I had several feeders hanging on the outer branches of a holly pruned in this way. The bare trunk allows the approach of a predator to be easily spotted by birds that are using the feeders. If the foliage on the tree is bushy enough and sufficiently high off the ground then the tree will also be used for nesting. The area under the holly requires fairly frequent clearing to remove seed debris and the occasional use of disinfectant to prevent avian diseases.

Above: *Winter can bring unusual visitors, like this Waxwing, to feed on berry crops.*

Right: *In winter Great Spotted Woodpeckers can be regular visitors to garden feeders.*

Bird tables and loose feeding

In order to satisfy the greatest number of birds, it is vital to continue to offer the food in a variety of ways. This will attract the widest range of bird species throughout the year.

Many species such as Dunnocks, Starlings, thrushes and various finches are most at home feeding on the ground, whereas canopy feeders such as Blue Tits and Great Tits will mostly use an elevated feeding station. The bird table can continue to be the main focus of your garden feeding station but food should also be presented on the ground. This may be much more difficult in winter, especially when there is snow about. Areas of the lawn or under trees need to be kept clear so that the ground-feeding birds can continue to get at the food. Provide as wide a range of food as possible, ranging from kitchen scraps to fruit. A supply of apples can be stored in autumn in a cool dark place and brought out to supplement other offerings in the middle of winter. These can be put out with other fruit that can often be bought cheaply when it has passed its best for human consumption. Peanuts can be put out but my preference is to crush them first – whole nuts are too much of an attraction to squirrels. Seeds can be scattered on the ground either onto grass or bare soil where stubble feeders such as Chaffinches can take advantage of them. These birds will also feed on the ground beneath hanging feeders to glean the seeds disturbed by the birds feeding above. If the trees in the garden are sufficiently old then a mixture of crushed nuts, seeds and fat can be wedged into cracks in the bark for tits, Treecreepers, Nuthatches and woodpeckers.

If space has permitted you to plant a small group of birches and alders then you can utilise the area underneath your little copse to grow spring woodland plants. The vegetation from these plants will die back in the summer and autumn leaving a clear space that

Left: *Birds such as thrushes will make good use of windfall or damaged apples. Surplus crops can be stored for use later in the year.*

can be used during the winter for loose feeding. An appropriate seed mix scattered on the soil will attract a range of ground feeders. The husks can be cleared up in late winter prior to the growing season. I had just such an area in my previous garden and it had two birches and an alder in a space about four yards square. Birches and Alders are fast growing, and reach a useful height within five years. I trained clematis and a climbing rose to grow up though the branches of the trees to add some gardening interest. When the trees are large enough the lower branches

should be pruned to give a secure feeding area and enough light for the woodland plants growing beneath the trees in the spring and early summer. In my current garden a line of old apple trees fulfils the same function, spring woodland plants grow underneath the trees which have feeders hanging from their outer branches. I have tried to encourage mistletoe to grow on the trees by collecting berries taken from trees elsewhere and squashing them into crevices in the bark.

Above: *Cold weather makes for a busy and crowded bird table and ground-feeders* (below) *take advantage of seeds spilt from hanging feeders or seeds scattered under trees and scrubs.*

For this to be successful the mistletoe must be taken from a tree of the same species. I have had no luck so far but know of a garden nearby where the technique has been successfully used.

Feeders

For obvious reasons the winter is the busiest time at a garden feeding station, particularly in late winter and during very cold spells.

You will find that at the periods of greatest demand the feeders will need refilling almost every day. This will happen even if some of your feeders are large with a big storage capacity. Somehow the word seems to get round the local bird community and often the only result of putting out larger feeders is that you will support more birds! Try to economize where possible and buy your seeds and nuts in bulk – quite good savings can be made.

This is the time of year to put out some of the more unusual types of feeders. Kitchen scraps can be contained in a close-mesh hanging basket that can be hung right amongst the trees. Suspend a section of gnarled tree trunk from a stout branch, having first drilled holes at intervals along its length. The cracks in the bark and these drilled holes can then be crammed with a mixture of crushed nuts and seeds held in a matrix of fat. (Vegetarians can use vegetable fat.) The branch that you hang up should be fairly heavy to minimize the amount of swinging and can be effective in attracting birds such as woodpeckers and Nuthatches. Hang feeders in a group, which will give the birds the feeling of feeding in a flock, bringing added security. Once the winter feeding regime has started. it is best to continue right through until spring without a break – this is especially important in very cold weather. If you are away for a few days then ask a neighbour to come into your garden and to replenish the feeders.

Below: *Hanging feeders come into their own with members of the tit family, but other, less acrobatic, bird species have learned to feed from them too.*

Water in the garden

Contrary to what you might think, the requirement for water is not greatly reduced in the winter. There might not be quite so much bathing taking place in the colder weather but it is still necessary for birds to maintain their feathers in good condition, so you still need to provide a supply of fresh water at all times.

Other sources of water that the birds might normally have access to could be frozen and the water that is made available in your garden could become very important.

There are several ways in which a bird bath can be kept ice-free. These range from using hot water to melt the ice to the use of a small immersion heater, although this might not be very practicable. Another method is to put a low-wattage light bulb under the bath, which will supply just enough heat to keep the bath ice-free. If the bird bath is made of a brittle material, a rubber ball can be placed in the water to take up the pressure from the expanding ice. This also gives a simple means of lifting out the ice once the ball has been removed from the water. Do not put any additives into the water to try to prevent it from freezing

If the birds in your garden depend on the pond for their winter water supply then there are some limitations on the methods available for keeping the pond ice-free. Very hot water should not be used to melt the ice as the thermal shock could kill some of the animal life, especially fish. Again, if fish are present, the ice should not be broken by banging hard on the surface as this also could harm them.

Above: *During a spell of hard weather, birds depend on an ice-free source of water.*

The best method is to place on the surface a large floating object such as a ball or a plastic washing-up bowl weighted with stones. When this is removed there will be a clear patch of water which will give access to the edge of the ice, it can then be removed. If it is not possible to clear the pond of ice or if the ice has become too thick, then some water should be made available in an alternative, smaller container such as a plastic dish. If a dish is used to supplement the water in your pond, remember to check it every day to keep it topped up and ice-free.

If you spread a net over your pond in the autumn, the leaves collected should be skimmed off every few weeks. Later in the winter, when the leaves have all fallen and many of those in the garden have been gathered for composting, the net can be removed. This will also allow frogs to start to return to your pond for spawning later in the winter and early spring.

Left: *Water supplies should be kept from freezing so birds can drink and clean their plumage, even if all natural sources are frozen.*

Cold weather movements

In addition to the regular seasonal migrations of many bird species, there are also large-scale movements caused by either unseasonal or exceptionally severe weather. When this happens, you might find unusual visitors at your feeding station such as Bramblings and Reed Buntings.

The winter thrushes will come into suburban gardens in greater numbers than usual. In a normal winter Redwings and Fieldfares start by feeding on invertebrates taken on the ground in fields and pastures. When supplies of these become scarce and harder to obtain because of frost they move on to strip the berries from the hedgerows, starting with Hawthorn and moving on to less attractive fruits such as rose-hips and ivy when the haws are finished, but still in rural areas. Large scale movements into towns and the suburbs of large cities take place when the berries are depleted in the wider countryside and in very tough times even berries such as cotoneaster will be taken. In a very mild winter this movement will scarcely take place at all and large flocks of thrushes can be found in rough pastures still feeding on invertebrates. Lapwings, pipits, skylarks and other birds of pastureland fly west and south. Often the movement of birds will involve birds flying into your region from areas that are currently much colder such as nearby continental Europe. Nor do these cold weather movements only involve land birds. In February 1979 a deep

Above: Winter thrushes such as Redwings visit the suburbs in greater numbers in cold weather in search for crops of berries.

Right: Siskins move into towns when food supplies in the country side diminish.

freeze over Scandinavia froze parts of the western Baltic Sea as well as all of the inland water bodies. This caused a large movement of scarce waterbirds such as Red-necked and Slavonian Grebes that flew into the country and were to be found on local lakes, reservoirs and ponds throughout Britain. In rural areas of the UK where there are flocks of geese and wild swans to be found feeding on agricultural land then garden based observers will be familiar with large flocks of these birds flying to and from favoured feeding areas. Insect eaters like wrens and robins find it exceptionally tough in these conditions and if the cold weather is sustained then mortality rates of some of the common birds can be very high.

Above: *Lapwings are frequently seen flying over in cold weather, seeking snow or frost-free fields.*

Right: *Common Gulls are widespread inland in winter and can be seen on farmland and urban areas like playing fields and lakes. Numbers can increase dramatically in cold weather.*

Pests and predators

In the winter, the threat to birds from domestic cats is somewhat reduced. The leaves have fallen from many of the trees and shrubs making the approach of a cat far easier to spot and cats naturally spend more time indoors.

The greatest dangers to birds in the winter and the main reasons for high mortality are a shortage of food and cold weather. Avian predators will take the occasional bird from your garden feeding station, but this is quite natural and is no reason to reduce the level of feeding. For some people, Sparrowhawks or, in towns, Kestrels may raid your garden bird population too frequently. If this is the case, try placing the feeders within the canopy of the trees and bushes, making it much more difficult for feeding birds to be taken. A couple of thick evergreen bushes will also help

by giving shelter, especially if they are prickly like Holly.

It is only when predators are not native or are found in unusually high numbers that they become a problem. Predation by domestic cats is at a much lower level than at other times of the year. Most cats prefer to be indoors in the warm during cold weather, fortunately this is when birds in the garden need to be left alone so that they can concentrate on feeding to build up their fat reserves for survival through the winter months.

Above: *Foxes in winter are pests rather than predators and will frequently come out after dark for scraps put out on the lawn for birds.*

Left: *Squirrels are mainly a nuisance for the damage they can do to feeders.*

Key winter species

Summer visitors have long since departed and been replaced by winter visitors in search of food. The importance of garden feeding stations, coupled with the bare vegetation, means that birds are often easier to see in winter. Add to this the fact that many species flock together in mixed feeding parties, and winter can become a very rewarding season for the garden birdwatcher.

LESSER SPOTTED WOODPECKER
Dendrocopos minor
Length: 14–15cm (5½–6in)

Resident. Tiny, sparrow-sized, with dumpy body and short tail, no red on vent. Male has a red crown.

The Lesser Spotted Woodpecker is not an easy bird to see at any time of the year. In the winter, it can be found moving through the topmost branches of the trees, foraging with a mixed flock of tits. It feeds on a range of invertebrate adults and larvae, including wood-boring beetles, spiders, and moth and butterfly larvae. For most of the winter they are silent but on a warm day in February, with no leaves yet on the trees, they can be located by their 'kee, kee, kee, kee' song and rapid drumming. The song has some similarity to the song of smaller raptors like the Kestrel. The 'kik' call and the drumming are both similar but more subdued than those of the Great Spotted Woodpecker. Both sexes drum and this is often delivered in two short bursts with a very short pause in between. Its unobtrusive nature means that this species is usually under-recorded. Its UK distribution is limited to the south and east of England, scarce in other parts. Lesser Spotted Woodpeckers prefer deciduous woodland habitat, parklands and old orchards, they are often associated with alders and watercourses. Lesser Spotted Woodpeckers are irregular and shy visitors to gardens and then only if the garden is adjacent to their preferred habitat. The species is a cavity nester, excavating a hole in a soft trunk or on a thicker branch. Nest boxes are also used. A single clutch of four to six pale eggs is laid in May, taking two weeks to incubate and a further three weeks to fledge.

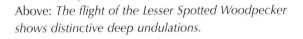

Above: *The flight of the Lesser Spotted Woodpecker shows distinctive deep undulations.*

Below: *The male Lesser Spotted Woodpecker is distinguished from the female by its red crown.*

WAXWING *Bombycilla garrulus*
Length: 17–18cm (6½–7in)

Winter visitor. Starling size, pinkish-buff, large crest, black bib and eye-mask, red and yellow marks on wing-tips and end of tail.

The Waxwing is a winter visitor from northern Scandinavian and western Siberian 'Taiga' forest areas to the eastern and central counties of Scotland and England. In most years there will be small numbers reported from late October and November onwards usually in eastern Scotland and north-eastern England. However, the species is prone to occasional periodic irruptions, linked to the cropping of the rowan tree in their breeding areas. Rowan berries are their staple food in Scandinavia, and in a good breeding year, with warm weather and a heavy crop of berries there will be good survival of young birds and a population peak. The irruption will take place the following year when the population is still high and the trees 'tired' resulting in a poor crop of berries. In these conditions, larger numbers of birds will cross the North Sea and flocks numbering several hundred may be seen in favoured east coast locations. In the UK, when they first arrive, Waxwings feed primarily on hawthorn berries but supplies of these are exhausted after a while and so stocks on the east coast will not last. Waxwings then start to move inland and into the outer suburbs of cities where they eat haws and also other berries from garden plants, especially cotoneaster. So, if you want Waxwings in your garden, move to the east coast from Norfolk northwards and plant lots of berry-bearing shrubs in your garden, especially hawthorn and cotoneaster!

Above right and above: *The Waxwing is one of the more exotic winter visitors to Britain. It feeds exclusively on berries, especially Hawthorn and Rowan.*

Right: *In flight Waxwings look similar to Starlings. They call frequently on the wing.*

WREN *Troglodytes troglodytes*
Length: 9–10cm (3½–4in)

Resident. Tiny, reddish-brown songbird with very short tail, often raised.

The Wren is one of the most wide-spread birds in the British Isles and also one of the most numerous. It is resident for the most part and the 1988-91 Atlas of Breeding Birds reported 7.1 million territories in Britain and 2.8 million in Ireland. In spite of these high numbers, Wrens could easily be overlooked were they not so noisy. When they are not singing or calling their habit of haunting the densest undergrowth makes them extremely difficult to see. They are common in or near gardens throughout their range and are found in towns and cities in all but the most built-up areas. In spite of being so common, they are not regular visitors to bird tables; crumbs or grated cheese scattered on the leaf litter under trees and bushes will be the best way of feeding Wrens. Nests are built in a variety of places – holes in trees, banks, piles of branches, ivy-covered walls. Artificial nest boxes are used, usually of the open-fronted design, but also on occasion a tit-box will be used. Communal roosting in nest boxes for warmth during winter months has been recorded. The male builds several nests, starting in early spring and then sings near-by to attract a female to it. The female lines the nest with feathers, hair and moss. In a year with plenty of food, two or three females might lay eggs within the territory of a single male. There are two

Above: *The Wren is one of Britain's smallest birds; the tiny tail accentuating its diminutive appearance.*

broods in most years, the first in late April or early May. Five or six white eggs are laid and take about two weeks to incubate. The young birds fledge after about seventeen days. The song of the Wren is probably the loudest for its size of any British bird; it consists of a series of metallic trills and loud notes and is usually delivered from cover.

Right: *The song is exceptionally loud for its size and can be heard almost all year round.*

Left: *Wrens will sometimes roost communally in nest boxes for winter warmth.*

FIELDFARE *Turdus pilaris*
Length: 24–27cm (9½–11in)

Winter visitor. A large handsome thrush with grey head and rump, streaked breast and chestnut back.

Fieldfares are primarily winter visitors to Britain and Ireland although a very small number breed here, mainly in upland areas. Their main breeding area is in Scandinavia, from where the majority of visitors to Britain arrive in early winter. The precise timing of their migration is linked to the availability of rowan berries; when there is a heavy crop the departure to the UK may be delayed until later in the winter. The Atlas of Wintering Birds (BTO, 1986) estimated that the British wintering population was about one million. They are often seen with other thrushes, in particular Redwings that arrive from Scandinavia and Iceland at about the same time. Initially, Fieldfares feed on the remnants of the berry crop, particularly hawthorn berries, but later in the winter they feed on invertebrates taken in open fields. During cold spells they also move into suburban areas and can be seen foraging for food

on large lawns and sports fields, especially just after a match has been played and the ground is disturbed. Orchards are also favourite places and they will feed on windfall apples and fruit rotting on the trees. They are known to defend a berry or fruit-laden tree from other birds. In gardens, they will take ornamental berries such as cotoneaster and pyracantha and can be attracted to fruit put out for them on the lawn. The call is a very distinctive 'chack, chack, chack' and is delivered both in flight and on the ground.

Above: Fieldfares are a common sight in open country in winter feeding on fruit and in berry bushes.

Left: Like most other thrushes Fieldfares feed chiefly on the ground, preferring invertebrates.

REDWING *Turdus iliacus*
Length: 20–22cm (8–9in)

Winter visitor. A small thrush with bold head markings, red flanks and underwings and a streaked breast.

The Redwing is a regular winter visitor to Britain and Ireland arriving at about the same time as the Fieldfare in late October and November. It is also a rare breeding bird in northern and western Scotland with less than a hundred breeding pairs in any year. It tolerates a wide range of breeding habitats although scrub is usually present, as are damp areas for feeding. It has a very distinctive flight call, a drawn out 'tsweeep', which can often be heard from an over-flying bird on a still night in October and November. It associates with Fieldfares and other thrushes in mixed feeding flocks and has similar dietary requirements to Fieldfares. Redwings feed on haws immediately after arriving and during the early part of the winter, but prefer to feed on invertebrates whenever conditions and the amount of frost allows. This is especially true in milder weather towards the end of the winter when large mixed flocks of Redwings, Starlings and other thrushes can be found feeding on damp pastureland. At times when the weather is cold they also feed by turning over leaf litter in woodland. It responds to adverse changes in the weather by moving into the outer suburbs and also by moving further west and south in search of more suitable areas for feeding. Redwings only really visit gardens when the weather is very cold in the middle of the winter. They are fussier than other thrushes and do not usually feed on the scraps put out on bird tables. They are also smaller than most thrushes and so come fairly low in the pecking order. Ensure your garden has some berry-bearing bushes, particularly hawthorn, available for them to feed from, scatter some apples out on the lawn and around the borders.

Above: *Redwings have a striking appearance, easily identified by their red flanks and distinctive eyestripe.*

Below: *Redwings are shyer than the larger thrushes and are dominated by them.*

MISTLE THRUSH *Turdus viscivorus*
Length: 26–28cm (10–11in)

Resident. A large thrush, grey-brown crown and upperparts, bold dark spots on whitish breast.

The Mistle Thrush is widespread in Britain and Ireland, only less common where trees are less frequent. It is absent from the Orkneys and Shetland and almost so from the Hebrides. The preferred habitat is open woodland and it is to be found also in parks, orchards and large gardens, both in deciduous trees and conifers. Mistle Thrushes do visit gardens and bird tables but are by no means common. The BTO *Garden BirdWatch Book* reports them from 10% or less of the gardens in most months of its survey. In winter, birds from northern Europe supplement the mainly resident population in England and Wales. There is some evidence that Scottish birds migrate west to Ireland in the winter. Mistle Thrushes defend larger territories than other thrushes and the reasons for this are not clear. It is an early nester and birds can be heard singing, often from high exposed perches from February onwards. The nest is placed either on a bough or, very frequently, in a fork of a tree and is made from grasses and plant material, strengthened with earth and lined with fine grasses. There are often two broods with the male continuing to feed the first brood while the female is laying the second clutch. The four eggs are either reddish-cream or greenish-blue speckled with brown and grey spots. Incubation takes two weeks and fledging slightly longer. The nests are very strongly defended from all types of potential predators – cats, other birds or even people that unknowingly stray too close to the nest. A wide range of insects and fruit is eaten, mostly invertebrates in the spring and summer, and berries in autumn and winter. Favourite berries are mistletoe, holly and yew. In the winter a food source such as a berry-bearing tree or a bird-table may be defended from other birds.

Left: *The Mistle Thrush sings from high, exposed perches.*

Below: *Mistle Thrushes are often seen feeding on invertebrates in the grass.*

Below: *The Mistle Thrush is larger, greyer and more boldly patterned than the smaller Song Thrush with a longer tail. Juveniles (left) are more heavily spotted and streaked on upperparts than adult birds.*

BLACKCAP *Sylvia atricapilla*
Length: 13–15cm (5–6in)

Resident/winter visitor. A medium-sized grey-brown warbler, male with a shaggy black cap. The cap is reddish-brown in female.

It might seem strange to include a warbler in a list of winter species but the results shown in the BTO *Garden BirdWatch Book* demonstrate clearly that this is the season when it is most often recorded in gardens. This is a trend that has become increasingly frequent over the past twenty or thirty years. Recent studies suggest that most of the Blackcaps in Britain and Ireland in winter are visitors from Continental Europe and that this may be a recently established habit. Although warblers are insectivorous and have the slim pointed bills typical of insectivores, the Blackcap's bill is fairly thick for a warbler and hence it is probably better able to cope with the range of food found in a winter garden feeding station. In the breeding season, Blackcaps ideally require well developed but airy woodland with a good understorey but they are also found in large gardens and areas of open scrub where there are tall trees which can be used as song perches. Also in the breeding season, they are noted as one of Britain's better songsters, with a squeaky initial warble developing into a melodic series of softly fluted notes. The song is not unlike that of the Garden Warbler and can cause some confusion. The distribution in Britain and Ireland shows England and Wales to be the stronghold, with a patchier distribution in Scotland and Ireland. The bulk of Britain's Blackcaps winter around the western Mediterranean and return for breeding in April and May.

Above: *Blackcaps are more often reported in gardens in winter than in summer.*

Right: *Blackcaps prefer to deliver their song from the cover of hedges or tall vegetation.*

The nest is built in bushes and hedgerows and is made from roots and grasses and lined with finer grass and hair. There are often two broods and the eggs are a buff colour with grey-brown blotching and are laid from mid-May onwards. Incubation is fast, taking only about eleven days. Fledging is also quick and takes from ten to thirteen days.

NUTHATCH *Sitta europaea*
Length: 13–14½cm (5–6in)

Resident. Small, compact birds with short tail and pointed bill, blue-grey above, rich buff beneath with rusty vent.

In Britain, the Nuthatch is common south of a line from the Wash to the Mersey. Even here it is absent from areas with few trees, such as the Fens. North of that line it is well established in Cumbria and the north-east and from here it is extending its range slowly northward. Its preference is for wooded areas that are part of forests or forest remnants rather than woodland areas in otherwise open country. It is mostly absent from all but the extreme south of Scotland and entirely from Ireland. In deciduous and mixed woods with a proportion of old oaks it can be quite common, and where these habitat requirements are met Nuthatches can be found in good numbers. In places Nuthatches are well established in parks and gardens but wherever they are found they are highly sedentary. The Nuthatch maintains a strict territory throughout the year and is an inveterate food hoarder. Knowledge of its quite small territory and of the food hoarded there is key to this behaviour. The species is very active and vocal, the song is a loud rapid trilling 'peeuw, peeuw, peeuw.......'. It feeds on insects, spiders, seeds and a variety of nuts and is a frequent visitor to bird tables where it can be quite dominant. In the garden, Nuthatches will feed on peanuts, sunflower seeds, bird cake and fatty mixtures smeared into tree trunks. The breeding behaviour is fascinating – the nest is built by the female and the entrance is reduced in size with mud until it is just large enough to admit her. The male then feeds her during egg laying and incubation. Incubation takes about two weeks and fledging a lengthy 23–25 days. Young birds become independent after a few days.

Above: *Nuthatches climb down tree trunks head first.*

Left: *In flight Nuthatches initially resemble small woodpeckers in shape and undulating flight.*

Below: *Nuthatch adjusts the entrance hole to its nest, plastering mud around it until it is the correct size.*

MAGPIE *Pica pica*
Length: 42–50cm (16½–20in)

Resident. Bold, noisy black and white member of crow family with very long tail.

The Magpie makes its presence known in gardens with its noisy, conspicuous behaviour and striking black and white plumage. It is widely distributed in England, Wales and Ireland but only locally common in Scotland. This is to a large extent due to persecution by gamekeepers in the nineteenth century; before this period it was more widely spread. To an extent persecution has diminished but numbers of Magpies still have not returned to their previous levels. However, in the main part of their range, numbers of Magpies have increased dramatically; in the past thirty years an increase of nearly 100% has been recorded. This increase is in part due to a decrease in keepering in England since the First World War but also a result of a dramatic spread into towns and cities in the past fifty years. With the exception of domestic cats and possibly crows, Magpies give the appearance of being the most significant predator of small birds in suburban gardens during the nesting season. However, studies show that nestlings and eggs make up only a small part of the Magpie's suburban diet and that the increase in their numbers has not had a marked effect on the breeding success of garden songbirds. Magpies operate a very effective defence system against a wide range of predators and intruders with their harsh alarm calls. A pair forms a breeding bond for life and the large enclosed oval stick-nest is placed in obvious locations, often in isolated trees and bushes, sometimes beside busy main roads. In the winter, especially, Magpies often form small flocks, gathering together in the evening to form communal roosts.

Above: *Magpies frequently gather in flocks in winter, with much noisy group interaction.*

Below: *Magpies have increased in towns and do take young birds, but have less impact on smaller species than is commonly thought.*

ROOK *Corvus frugilegus*
Length: 44–47cm (17–18½in)

Resident. Large all-black crow with long bill having distinctive pale grey base.

The Rook is widespread throughout Britain and Ireland, missing only from the central and north-western parts of Scotland. It is a bird of open and cultivated land and does not venture into the larger towns or cities. It is not a common garden visitor and will only be known in larger country gardens that are situated near a rookery. A wide range of food is eaten, including many farming pests such as leatherjackets, and Rooks are often to be seen waddling around fields foraging on short grass and stubble. Other food includes beetles, worms, caterpillars, insects, grain and fruit. In common with other crow species, Rooks rob nests of eggs and young birds. They are social birds, nesting colonially and often feeding in flocks. The rookery is built in the tops of a group of tall trees and the nests are messily constructed of twigs, grasses and mud and are lined with finer grasses and bits of plant. The rookery is occupied and buzzing with activity before the end of the winter, when the trees are still bare. Nesting takes place from February to June. A single clutch of three to five greenish speckled eggs are laid and incubated for sixteen to eighteen days. Fledging takes from 32–33 days. Rooks are noisy birds both at the rookery and when in feeding flocks; the commonest call is a nasal 'kaaah' and the song is a cackling mixture of croaks, rattles and soft caws.

Above: *Rooks are colonial nesters in copses or on the edge of woodland, feeding in nearby fields.*

Left: *Adult birds are easily recognised by their whitish bills.*

SISKIN *Carduelis spinus*
Length: 11.5–12.5cm (4½–5in)

Resident/winter visitor. A small finch, green and yellow, male with a black cap, female a drab grey-green.

The Siskin is a locally common breeding bird in the British Isles and a winter visitor from northern and eastern Europe during the winter months, sometimes in huge numbers. As a breeding bird it is confined to coniferous plantations in the north and west of Britain and Ireland, especially spruce. It is primarily a feeder on tree seeds and in the winter it feeds especially on the seeds from alder and birch trees. It has increased in numbers as a breeding bird and as a winter visitor quite recently. Its habit of visiting gardens and feeding on peanuts during winter and early spring was first reported on in 1963. Visiting birds arrive en masse from October onwards and for the first part of the winter they feed on tree seeds in relatively open woodland, moving into gardens when the natural food sources become exhausted. They stay quite late and are often still present at the end of April or early in May, at this time they can frequently be heard singing and displaying. Their main food in gardens is peanuts and they are supposed especially to like the nuts when presented in red plastic mesh. However, if squirrels are present, this is quite impossible, and normal feeders are perfectly acceptable to Siskins. Breeding takes place in conifer plantations where a nest is constructed from lichens and small twigs and lined with hair, moss and feathers. The nest is usually placed high in a spruce tree near the end of a branch. There are often two broods and between three to five pale blue, red-streaked eggs are laid in May. Incubation takes 12 days and fledging a further fifteen days. Calls are often given in flight, and the most common are an upward inflected 'tsooeee' and a downward inflected 'teelew'. The song is a prolonged series of trilling and twittering notes interrupted by a drawn-out wheezing note.

Above: *Siskins are reputed to be attracted to red plastic mesh feeders.*

Below: *Siskins often feed on birch and alder catkins.*

REDPOLL *Acanthis flammea*
Length: 11.5–13cm (4½–5in)

Winter visitor. Small grey and brown finch with small black bib and red forehead, breast in breeding male pinkish red.

The Redpoll often associates with the Siskin in winter feeding parties on alders and birches. In Britain it is a breeding partial migrant and a winter visitor. It breeds in birch woodland and young conifer plantations and is distributed throughout Britain and Ireland wherever this habitat occurs. At the time of the earlier BTO Breeding Atlas it was increasing rapidly in numbers. Since then, the population has markedly decreased. This is thought to be due primarily to the changing age structure of conifers in Britain

Above: *Redpolls share a liking for alder seeds with Siskins.*

and also to a reduction in the number of birches as a result of natural succession. In the past twenty years there has been less planting and a consequent reduction in the younger plantations that the species prefers. The Redpoll is not a frequent visitor to gardens unless they are close to areas of silver birch. Any visits are usually brief as Redpolls are very mobile. The call, often given in flight as a flock flies overhead, is a repetitive and metallic 'chew, chew, chew'. The song is also often delivered in flight. There are several different races of Redpoll and they can differ appreciably in size. This can be seen in the winter when a large flock is encountered or passes through. Breeding is not generally in an area with gardens and takes place from late May. There are usually two clutches of four to six bluish-white eggs with red blotches. Incubation takes from ten to twelve days and fledging another nine to eleven days.

Top left: *Redpolls in flight are best identified by their distinctive call.*

Above and right: *The male Redpoll (right) has a bright red breast in summer plumage.*

HAWFINCH *Coccothraustes coccothraustes*
Length: 16–17cm (6–6½in)

Resident. A large finch with massive bill, russet head, grey nape, dark brown back, white bar on wing.

This species is extremely shy and its British breeding and winter distribution is confined to a sparse scattering in England and in Wales. It is probably under-recorded owing to its unobtrusive nature, although once you are familiar with its calls, it becomes somewhat easier to locate.

It breeds in deciduous and mixed woodland, preferring mature tall trees in particular beech, hornbeam and oak. It can also be found in parks, large wooded gardens and orchards. Its diet changes with the seasons and consists of seeds, fruits, buds and insects. With its massive bill, it is able to crack open fruit stones such as cherry. In woodland it is often in the canopy during the spring and then it is more often heard than seen flying across gaps between the trees. The call is an explosive hard 'zik' or 'tic' and can be heard from a considerable distance. In winter, it tends to move into suburbs and gardens only in the colder weather and in common with other finches it will feed on berries such as cotoneaster, berberis and honeysuckle. It nests from late April

Above: *The broad white wing-bar and white tail band are evident in flight.*

onwards in fruit trees or bushes and builds its nest on a base of twigs that it lines with mosses, lichens and hair. The eggs are bluish or grey-green spotted and streaked with dark brown. Incubation and fledging both take about ten days.

The male Hawfinch (below, left) *has a richer plumage colour than the female* (below, right).

ful addresses and further reading

Field Guides

The Collins Bird Guide, Lars Svennsson, Peter J. Grant, Killian Mullarney and Dan Zetterström (Collins, 2001)

New Holland European Bird Guide, Peter H. Barthel and Paschalis Dougalis (New Holland, 2008)

Further Reading

All About ... Garden Wildlife, David Chandler (New Holland, 2008)

Attracting Birds to your Garden, David Cottridge and Stephen Moss (New Holland, 2000)

The Complete Garden Bird Book, Mark Golley, Stephen Moss and Dave Daly (New Holland, 2001)

Cooking for Birds, Mark Golley (New Holland, 2006)

Garden BirdWatch Handbook, A. Cannon (BTO, 2nd ed. 2000)

Gardenwatch, Sarah Whittley (New Holland, 2008)

The Ultimate Birdfeeder Handbook, John A. Burton (New Holland, 2006)

References

The Atlas of Breeding Birds in Britain & Ireland, 1988–1991, Gibbons, Reid, Chapman (T & AD Poyser, 1993)

The Atlas of Wintering Birds in Britain & Ireland, Lack (T & AD Poyser, 1986)

Magazines

Birdwatch Available from larger newsagents or by subscription from: Birdwatch subscriptions, WarnersGroup Publications, West Street, Bourne, Lincolnshire PE10 9PH, UK. Tel: 01778 392027

Organisations

The Wildlife Trusts, The Kiln, Waterside, Mather Road, Newark, Nottinghamshire NG24 1WT
Tel: 01636 677711, Fax: 01636 670001
E-mail: info@wildlife-trusts.cix.co.uk
Website: www.wildlifetrust.org.uk

Cat/Fox Deterrents, Catwatch Concept Research, Unit 9, Bowmans Trading Estate, Bessemer Drive, Stevenage, Hertfordshire, SG1 2D
Tel: 01438 727183, Fax: 01438 350918
E-mail: main@conceptresearch.demon.co.uk
Website: www.conceptresearch.co.uk

The British Trust for Ornithology (BTO), The Nunnery Thetford Norfolk IP24 2PU UK Tel: 01842 750050
E-mail: gbw@bto.org

The Royal Society for the Protection of Birds (RSPB), The Lodge, Sandy, Bedfordshire SG19 2DL UK
Tel: 01767 680551 Website: http://www.rspb.org.uk
www.rspb.org.uk

Tree Advice Trust, Alice Holt Lodge, Farnham, Surrey GU10 4LH
Tel: 01420 22022 Fax: 01420 22000
Tree Advice Helpline 09065 161147
E-mail: admin@treehelp.info
Website: www.treeahelp.info

Bird food suppliers

CJ WildBird Foods, The Rea, Upton Magna, Shrewsbury, Shropshire SY4 4UB Tel: 0800 731 2820
Website: http://www.birdfood.co.uk
www.birdfood.co.uk

John E Haith, Park Street, Cleethorpes, Lincs DN35 7NF, Tel: 01472 357515

Glossary

Aquatic plant A plant located entirely in the water, either rooted to the bottom or floating.

Avian Of a bird – an avian predator is a bird of prey or an owl.

Bird bath A receptacle for water, sometimes on a pedestal, usually less than 60 cm across.

Bird table A platform for feeding birds, often of wood, up to 60 cm across, mounted on a pole about 1.5 m above the ground.

Broadleaf Tree A tree other than a conifer – many are deciduous, loosing their leaves in the winter.

Brood Young birds from a single clutch of eggs

Call A social noise, usually short, made by a bird, for a variety of reasons, such as alarm or contact.

Cover Area of safety from predators, a shrub or tree with leaves, also vegetation on the ground.

Display Attractive behaviour in the breeding season, intended to secure a mate.

Feral Existing in a wild state, having previously been domesticated.

Fledgling A young bird hatched but not yet capable of flight.

Incubation The period after laying when the eggs are kept warm by adult birds, prior to hatching.

Irruption A periodic mass movement of birds, in response to a physical stimulus, food shortage or bad weather.

Juvenile A young bird in its first full plumage after hatching.

Loose feed Food made available on the ground or on a table – not in a container.

Marginal plants Water plants growing on the edge of the pond or in very shallow water along the edge.

Migrant A bird undertaking a seasonal movement to another place for breeding or food.

Nest hole A hole in a tree trunk or main branch used by cavity nesting bird.

Nest box An artificial nest site, with either open or hole entrance, size depending on species.

Nut feeders A container for the controlled dispensing of peanuts, usually filled from a closeable top.

Oxygenators Water plants specifically for oxygenating the water, usually submerged, rooted or free.

Predator An animal or bird killing another for food.

Raptor A bird of prey: kestrel, buzzard, eagle, etc.

Sahel An arid region to the south of the Sahara extensively used by migrants.

Scrub A stage in the natural succession of vegetation, consisting of shrubs and herbaceous plants.

Seed feeders A container for the controlled dispensing of seeds of various types.

Song A mostly musical collection of notes used mainly during breeding to advertise for a mate and to maintain territory. Unique to a species or sub-species.

Species A distinct population of one type of bird which cannot interbreed with other unique types.

Sub-species An isolated population within a species showing different characters, such as call or plumage, but still capable of successful interbreeding.

Summer visitor A bird spending the winter usually further south and coming to the UK to breed or over-winter (applies to some southern hemisphere seabirds).

Taiga Northern hemisphere coniferous forests circling the globe, Scandinavia, Russia and Canada.

Tundra Northern hemisphere boggy fens, peat-bogs and fells, north of the taiga.

Wildlife Gardening Gardening intended to create habitat within the garden suitable for wildlife.

Winter visitor A bird spending the winter in the UK having bred further north or east.

Index

Page numbers in **bold** refer to illustrations.

Author's Acknowledgements

I would like to thank Jo Hemmings at New Holland for her encouragement and ideas at the start of the project and also Mike Unwin at New Holland for his enthusiasm and help during the writing of the manuscript and through the various stages of the editorial process. Dominic Mitchell gave invaluable help and advice gathered from his wide publishing experience. I would also like to thank Erica Laurentius and my mother, Gwen Beddard for encouraging my interest in gardening over a period of many years. On the birding side I would like to remember the encouragement given to me by the late Jim Ireland when I was getting back into birding over 25-30 years ago. This, after a lapse during late teenage and college years when there were other distractions. Staff at CJWildbird Foods Ltd have been helpful with advice on feeding and letting me trial a new feeder. Ian Dawson at the RSPB and Andrew Cannon at the BTO (Garden BirdWatch) both provided useful information during the writing stage.

Photographic Acknowledgements

All photographs by David M. Cottridge, with the exception of the following:

Frank Blackburn (Windrush Photos), p41; p43
Les Borg, p39; p99
Richard Brooks (Windrush Photos), p28
R. J. Chandler (Windrush Photos), p105(b)
Bill Coster (Windrush Photos), p76
Michael Gore, p107
Dennis Green (Windrush Photos), p29; p36; p46; p48
John Hollis (Windrush Photos), p88; p91
David Kjaer, p3(t); p4; p14(t); p62; p69; p74(b); p96; p123(bl)
Gordon Langsbury, p116
Tim Loseby, p121; p123(br)
Mark Lucas (Windrush Photos), p26(t)
George McCarthy (Windrush Photos), p59
Alan Petty (Windrush Photos), p34
Richard Revels, p17; p20; p77(b)
David Tipling, p45; p52; p66; p73; p87; p97; p105(t); p117
Chris Whittles, p75
Alan Williams, p19(t); p22(b); p33; p84; p86; p95; p98; 109
Markus Varesvuo, front cover
Roger Wilmshurst, p68; p79; p108
Marcus Young (Windrush Photos), p25(t)

(t= top; b=bottom; c=centre; l=left; r=right)